To

From

To Steve   S.P.

Text by Sophie Piper
Illustrations copyright © 2015 Ruth Rivers
This edition copyright © 2015 Lion Hudson

Published by Lion Children's Books
an imprint of
Lion Hudson plc
Wilkinson House, Jordan Hill Road,
Oxford OX2 8DR, England
www.lionhudson.com/lionchildrens

ISBN 978 0 7459 6400 3

First edition 2015

Acknowledgments
Scripture quotations are taken or adapted from the Good News Bible © 1994 published by the Bible Societies/HarperCollins Publishers Ltd UK, Good News Bible© American Bible Society 1966, 1971, 1976, 1992. Used with permission.

The Lord's Prayer as it appears in Common Worship: Services and Prayers for the Church of England (Church House Publishing, 2000) is copyright © The English Language Liturgical Consultation and is reproduced by permission of the publisher.

A catalogue record for this book is available from the British Library

Printed and bound in Singapore, July 2015, LH18

THE LION
STORY
BIBLE

Words by Sophie Piper

Pictures by Ruth Rivers

LION
CHILDREN'S

Contents

THE NEW TESTAMENT   120

THE OLD TESTAMENT

The Old Testament is the first part of the Christian Bible. It is a collection of writings that the Jews have revered as their holy scriptures since ancient times. Jesus himself knew and loved them.

The collection opens with stories of the very beginning: stories about the God who made the world and everything in it; stories about the relationship between God and humankind; stories of human foolishness in turning away from their Maker.

Other writings tell the story of God's plan to rebuild the broken friendship with humankind. They tell of how, long ago, God chose a man named Abraham to be the father of

a special nation: one who would obey God's laws and bring God's blessing to all the world.

The family of Abraham grew and grew, and in time became the nation known as the Jews. Time and again God showed them the good and right way to live. Time and again they let God down... through disobedience, through forgetfulness, through weakness.

Time and again God forgave his people. Holy prophets came and spoke messages of hope: one day, God would send a saviour. One day.

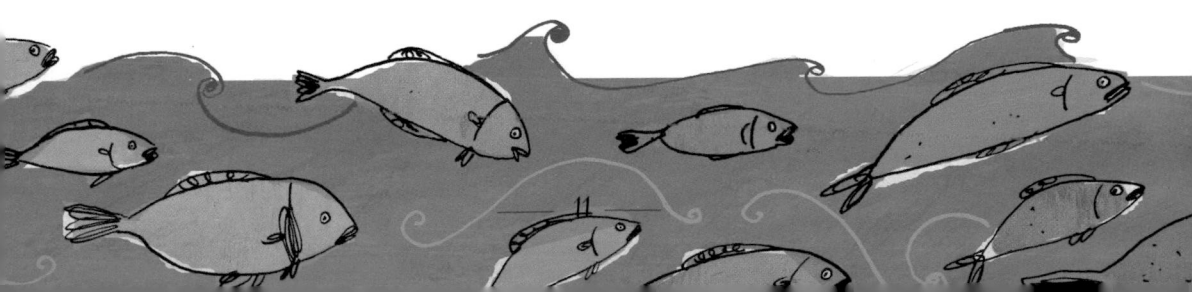

FROM DARK

Before the beginning, there was nothing:
a dark, shapeless nothing
and God.

Then God spoke:
"Let there be light."
And there was:
the light of the very first day.

On the second day, God made the sky
above and the sea below.

Next, God called the land from out of the sea and all kinds
of plants began to grow upon it.

The golden light of the sun warmed the earth in daytime.
The silver moon lit the night, and millions of stars twinkled
in the heavens.

God made the creatures that lived in the sea: the darting
fish, the plunging monsters, the things half
seen in the ripples.

TO LIGHT

God also made the many birds that soared and flitted and shrieked and twittered.

And God made all the animals: the huge and lumbering elephants, the tiny shrews, the wild and fearsome lions, and the gentle, obedient cattle.

Everything God had made was astonishing, amazing, and absolutely perfect.

PEOPLE

Last of all, God made people.

"I give you my blessing,"
God told them. "I am putting you in
charge of everything I have made.
"I want you, and your children, and your children's
children to take care of this world for always."
Now the six days of making the world were done.
"The seventh day will be special," said God.
"It will be a day of rest and enjoyment for all
of my creation."

God named the first man "Adam", and the first woman "Eve".

The Garden of Eden was their paradise home.

"Everything here is for you to enjoy," said God. "The trees are heavy with fruit, and it hangs low for you to pick.

"There is just one tree you must not touch. Its fruit will open your eyes to all kinds of evil.

"If you eat it, you will die."

Why would Adam and Eve even think to disobey? God had given them all they needed to be happy.

FORBIDDEN FRUIT

One day, Eve heard a whisper.

"Look at this delicious fruit! Why did God tell you not to eat it?"

"Because it will poison us," replied Eve.

"I know better," said the snake. "God knows it will make you wise... and God doesn't want that."

Eve wondered. The fruit did look appealing. She tried some. It was delicious. She gave some to Adam.

And as they ate, they began to see everything differently.

First of all, they saw that they were naked and they felt SO embarrassed. They hurried to make clothes from leaves.

BANISHED

In the evening, God came to talk to Adam and Eve. But now they felt ashamed that they had not obeyed God, and they hid.

But God soon found them.

"So you disobeyed," said God. "You cannot stay in paradise any longer.

"Life will be hard in the world beyond.

"I will give you animal skins for clothing, but for food you will have to farm the land."

As Adam and Eve left Paradise, they saw an angel with a fiery sword at the gate.

Was there no way back? How could they be friends with God again?

CAIN AND ABEL

Adam and Eve's firstborn baby was a boy. They named him "Cain".

Their next baby was another boy: they named him "Abel".

When Cain grew up, he became a farmer. Abel became a shepherd.

The time came when they each decided to bring an offering to God. Cain brought some of his harvest crops. Abel brought a lamb and killed it as a sacrifice.

God was pleased with what Abel did, but rejected what Cain did.

Then came the real problem: Cain got angry. Very angry.

"Watch out," said God. "That temptation to do the wrong thing is right next to you, waiting to pounce."

Cain paid no attention to the warning.

"Let's go out into the fields," he said to Abel in a careless kind of way.

When they were out and alone, Cain killed Abel. He watched the blood trickle into the ground.

But God had seen everything.

"This blood-soaked land will no longer grow crops for you," said God. "Go now: you will be a homeless wanderer for ever."

NOAH AND THE ARK

Years went by, and the number of people on earth grew and grew.

But they also grew more wicked. God became very weary of their fighting.

So God made a plan. Then he went and spoke to the one good man left: Noah.

"I want you to build a huge boat – an ark. On it I want you to take your family and a pair of every kind of animal.

"I am going to send a flood to wash away the world's wickedness.

"You and the ark will be safe, and able to start the whole world anew."

20

THE FLOOD

Noah built the ark as God had asked. Once he was safe on board with his family and the animals, God sent the rain.

It rained as never before. The flood rose up. It drowned the whole wide world.

For days and weeks the ark floated on the water, higher than the highest hills...

Until one day – CRUNCH. It stuck fast on a mountaintop.

Noah sent out a raven to look for land. It flapped and flapped and flew around. But then it simply flew away.

A little later, Noah sent out a dove. It flew until it was just a speck – and not even that. Then – oh joy! It flew back with a fresh green olive twig. Somewhere the land was dry!

A RAINBOW AND A PROMISE

At long last, the floodwater went down.

"It's time to leave the ark," said God to Noah. "Set the animals free. They must have young and make their homes in this bright new world.

"And here's more good news: your sons and their wives will have children, and so there will be people in my world again.

"Now look – there is my rainbow in the sky. Whenever you see it, remember the promise I am making.

"I will never send a flood like that again.

"From now on there will always be summer and winter, seedtime and harvest, cold and heat, day and night."

THE TOWER OF BABYLON

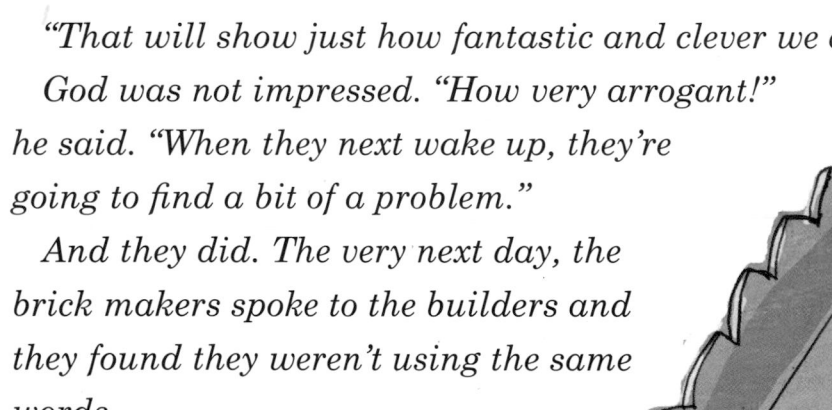

*I*n the beginning, all the people in the world spoke the same language.

The time came when they made their home on a wide plain in a place called Babylonia. There, they discovered how to make strong bricks from the clay by the river.

"We can build anything we like with bricks," they exclaimed to one another.

"We could build a tower so tall it will reach the sky.

"That will show just how fantastic and clever we are!"

God was not impressed. "How very arrogant!" he said. "When they next wake up, they're going to find a bit of a problem."

And they did. The very next day, the brick makers spoke to the builders and they found they weren't using the same words.

And the cooks seemed to have some gobbledygook of their own.

In no time at all, the people split into little groups, each
with their own special language. No one could agree on
anything, let alone a tower. And off they went, to every corner
of the world.

GOD'S PEOPLE

Long ago there lived a man named Abram. He had been born and raised in the city.

So it was a surprise when God gave him this message:

"Abram, I want you to take your family and travel to a new land. It will be a home for your family now and always.

"You will have many descendants and they will become a nation. Through them, I will bless the world."

Abram obeyed. With his wife Sarai, his nephew Lot, his many servants, and everything he owned, he set out for the land of Canaan.

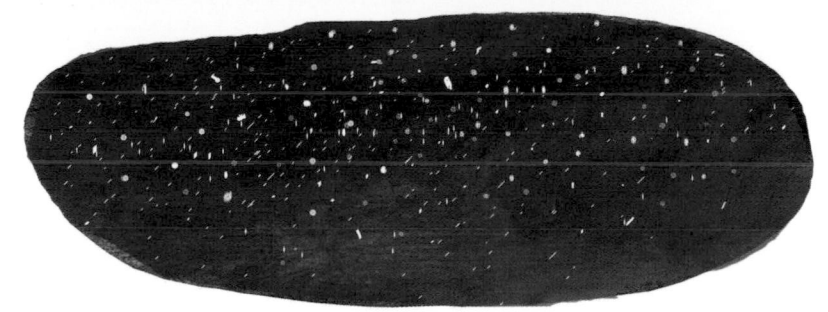

ONE STARRY NIGHT

I n the land of Canaan, Abram lived as a nomad, making his
camp wherever he could find pasture for his flocks.
He grew very wealthy.

One thing troubled him. He and his wife had no children.
One day he would die, and he would have to leave all he had
to a slave.

Then God led him outside. "Look up at the
night sky," said God. "One day, your family
will be as many as the stars."

In spite of his sadness, Abram
still trusted God.

27

SODOM AND GOMORRAH

Abram's nephew Lot had also prospered in the land of Canaan. Both men had huge flocks of sheep, goats, and cattle.

The trouble was, it was hard to find enough pasture for all the animals. For this reason Abram and his nephew had agreed to part.

Lot made his home in the valley of the River Jordan, and the city of Sodom. He did not really fit in. The people in Sodom and the nearby city of Gomorrah were wicked and violent.

One day, two strangers came to the city. Lot invited them to stay the night. A mob came and hammered on the door, demanding to take advantage of the two men. Lot refused.

"You must flee this place!" warned the strangers. "God is going to destroy these wicked cities.

"Hurry – gather all your family and together we will run for our lives. And don't look back."

They had barely reached a place of safety when disaster struck.

Burning sulphur fell like rain on Sodom and Gomorrah.

Lot's wife turned to look. At once she became a pillar of salt.

29

ABRAHAM

*Y*ears went by, and still Abram had no son.

"Do not despair," said God. "I name you Abraham, meaning 'father of many'. Your wife will be Sarah, 'the mother of nations'."

At long last God's promise came true, Abraham and Sarah had a baby boy. They named him Isaac, and the word means "laughter".

AND ISAAC

Some years after that, God tested Abraham.

"Take your son," said God, "and everything you need to offer an animal as a burned sacrifice.

"Go to a high mountain and build an altar with firewood on top.

"Then tie up your son, throw him on top, and kill him before setting him alight."

Abraham obeyed all he believed God had said. Who can tell what he was thinking as he raised the knife.

Then God spoke again. "Don't harm the boy. You have shown you respect me more than anyone."

Abraham saw a goat trapped in the thorns. He knew that this was the sacrifice God wanted.

"Because of your obedience, I promise to bless you and your family for ever," said God.

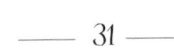

— 31 —

THE CHEATER

Isaac grew up and married Rebecca. Their twin sons were Esau and Jacob.

From the very start, Jacob was jealous.

"Esau is only a tiny bit older than me," he complained, "but that means he's in line for the best of everything."

He began to think cheating thoughts.

One day, when Esau came home hungry from hunting, Jacob made this offer:

"A bowl of soup in exchange for your rights as the eldest," he said.

Too hungry to think, Esau agreed.

Later, when Isaac was old and couldn't see well, Jacob dressed up so that he looked and felt like Esau. "Give me the blessing due to the firstborn son," he asked.

Isaac did so.

And that made Esau furious. "I'll kill that cheat," he shouted.

...GETS CHEATED

Jacob ran for his life: miles and miles to his Uncle Laban.

Wily old Uncle Laban! He agreed to let Jacob marry his lovely daughter Rachel... in exchange for years of work without pay.

As Jacob tended the flocks of sheep and goats, he worked out how to get even.

"Let me just have the black lambs and kids that are born striped or speckled," he pleaded, and Laban agreed.

To Laban's astonishment, Jacob made sure that nearly all the newborn sheep were black and the goats were striped or speckled. Jacob grew very, very wealthy.

It was no surprise when the two cheats fell out and Jacob set off for home.

WHEN JACOB

J acob set out on the long walk back to Canaan.
He had with him his wives and his children and his
servants and his fighting men and his flock of sheep and his
flocks of goats and all the other animals he owned…

And one more thing as well.

A very big problem.

There was no way of avoiding it. He was going to have
to meet his brother Esau. The brother he had cheated. The
brother who had vowed to kill him in revenge. The brother
who even now, his servants had warned him, was coming to
meet him with four hundred fighting men.

MET ESAU

Jacob made a plan. He chose some of the best of his goats and sheep and camels and cows and bulls, and divided them into smaller herds.

Then he put servants in charge of each herd and sent them off one group at a time to meet Esau and to declare that the animals were a gift.

But the moment of meeting could not be avoided. And now it was upon him – and Esau was running toward him.

Esau hugged his brother Jacob and kissed him. He wasn't interested in the gifts.

He just wanted to be friends with his brother.

THE AMAZING COAT

J oseph knew he was special.

His father, Jacob, had twelve sons, and ten of them were older than Joseph.

But he had chosen Joseph to have all the privileges of the eldest.

And how did Joseph know that? Because his father had given him a fabulously wonderful look-at-me coat.

Did it make Joseph's brothers just a little bit jealous?

Yes, it did.

DREAM ON

One night, Joseph had a dream. In the morning, he told his brothers about it.

"Listen: we were all in the field gathering in the harvest. My sheaf stood up in the middle. Your sheaves gathered around in a circle and bowed down.

"Interesting, don't you think?"

"No, it's not interesting," replied his brothers. "And if you think it means we're going to bow down to you and your coat, dream on."

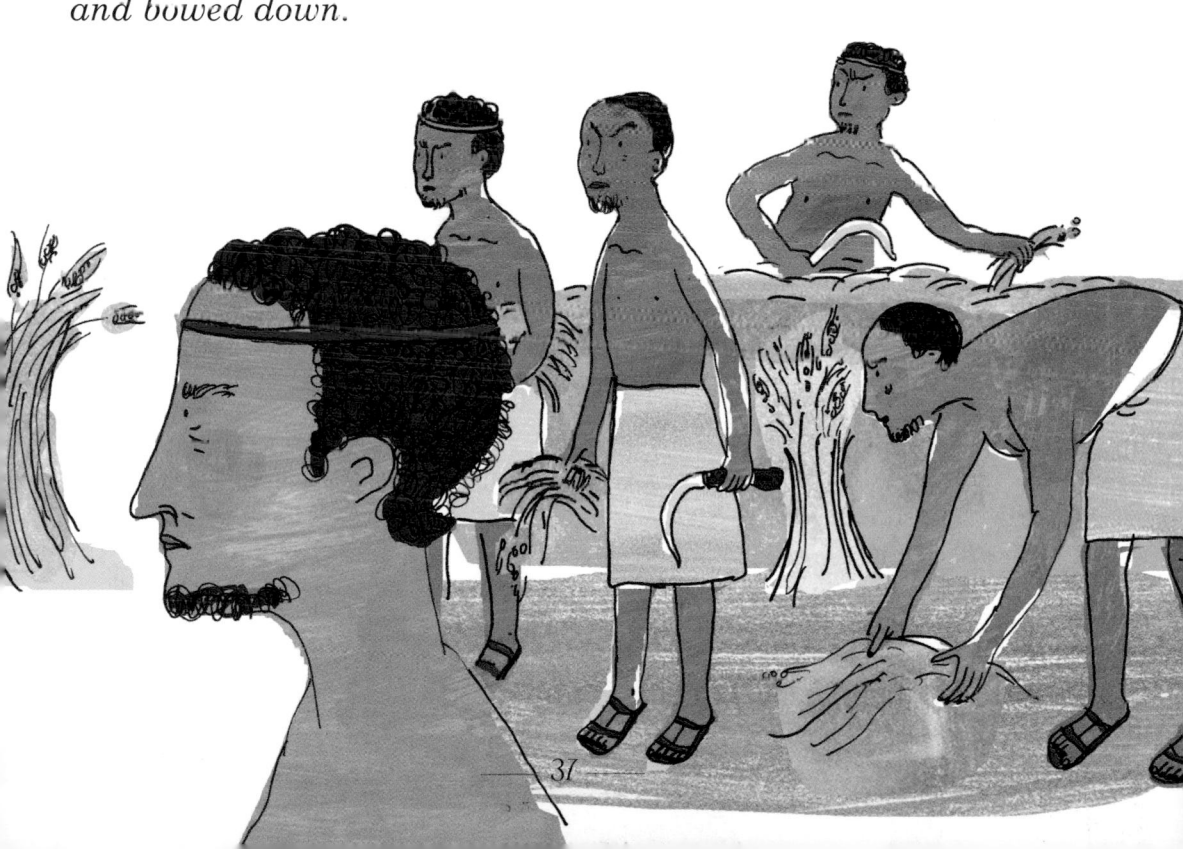

31

JOSEPH IN TROUBLE

O ne day, Joseph's brothers turned against him.
They ripped off his coat and sold him to traders who were passing by.

They dipped the coat in blood and took it back to Jacob.
"A wild animal must have got him," they lied.
The traders took Joseph to Egypt and sold him as a slave. Though he worked hard and honestly, someone told lies about him and had him thrown into jail.

But God was still looking after Joseph and gave him the wisdom to explain dreams.

The king's butler was among the prisoners, and he had a strange dream.

"I saw myself squeezing grapes into the king's cup," he said.

"It means you will soon be back in your old job," explained Joseph. "When you are, remember me."

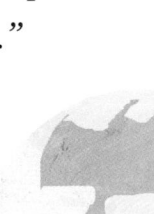

And so it turned out. When the king had puzzling dreams, the butler said to send for Joseph.

The prisoner was brought.

"Listen," said the king. "First I saw seven fat cows clamber up from the river and begin grazing. Then seven thin cows came and ate them.

"Next I saw seven fat ears of grain. Then seven thin ears came and ate them.

"I don't know what it all means. My advisors don't know what it all means. My question is this: do you?"

HARVEST AND FAMINE

J oseph listened hard as the king told his two dreams.

"They both mean the same thing," he said. "There will be seven years of good harvests, and then seven years of bad harvests.

"You must choose someone to store the abundance of the good years to last through the famine."

"I will," said the king. "I choose you."

So it was. When the famine struck, Joseph was the man in charge of selling grain to those who had none.

People came from far away. One day, ten men arrived from Canaan. They gathered around the great man and bowed down low.

Joseph recognized them at once: they were his brothers!

The scoundrels who had so mistreated him... but still his brothers. And they hadn't recognized him. Whatever should he do?

JOSEPH AND HIS BROTHERS

J oseph made a plan.

He asked the brothers to tell him about their family.

He found out that his younger brother, Benjamin, was alive and well, and he demanded that they bring him on their next visit.

When the brothers returned with Benjamin to buy more grain, Joseph ordered his servants to fill their packs.

And he secretly ordered that a silver goblet be slipped into Benjamin's pack.

After the brothers had set out for home, Joseph sent his servant to chase them down.

"My master's precious goblet is missing!" he cried. "The one who is the thief will have to stay as my master's slave.

"Ah – it's the young lad!"

The ten older brothers refused to
abandon Benjamin. When they were
brought to Joseph, the one named
Judah stepped forward.

"Let Benjamin go back to our
father Jacob," he said. "He reminds him
of another son, Joseph, who is dead. They were
the two sons of his much-loved wife Rachel.

"Make me your slave instead."

It was then that Joseph knew: his brothers were sorry
for what they'd done to him so many years before.

"I'm Joseph," he cried. "God has
made everything turn out right.
What you did then means I can
help you all now."

And he invited them to fetch
the whole family and come to
Egypt.

SLAVES IN EGYPT

When Joseph invited his family to Egypt, they were made welcome. Their children prospered, and their children's children. As the years went by they became a nation: the people of Israel.

Then a new king came to power. He didn't know about Joseph and he didn't care.

What bothered him was having tribes of foreigners living in his country.

"They might cause trouble," he told his officials, "and decide they don't want to live by our rules.

"So let's solve the problem now – let's make them our slaves.

"I've got some big ideas for new cities, and what I need is lots of bricks.

"That means brick makers.

"Set those Israelites to work."

And he appointed cruel slave-drivers to make sure that his orders were obeyed.

THE BABY

The king of Egypt had made the Israelites his slaves.

But he still fretted. "There are too many being born," he said. "I order my people to seek out their baby boys and drown them in the river."

But one mother would not give in. "We will make a basket to be a floating cradle," she told her daughter Miriam.

"We will hide your baby brother in it, among the reeds at the water's edge."

Miriam stayed to watch the cradle.

...AND THE PRINCESS

A princess of Egypt came down to bathe.
She saw the basket.

"Please fetch it for me," she told a servant.
Then she lifted the lid and saw
"A BABY!

"I shall keep him safe," she declared.
"And I shall give him the name I choose: 'Moses'."

Miriam stepped forward. "I know someone who
could look after that baby for you," she said.

She went and fetched her mother!

FROM PRINCE

Moses grew up as a prince in Egypt. However, he knew he had been born an Israelite, and as a young man he was curious to see how his people lived.

He was dismayed to see how hard they had to work. He was angry at the way the slave-drivers whipped and beat them.

One slave-driver was so violent that he killed a slave. In a sudden rage, Moses took revenge and killed him. But others saw his crime. Moses had to flee.

TO SHEPHERD

Moses found a welcome in the land of Midian. He joined the household of Jethro and worked as his shepherd, leading the flocks of sheep and goats to wherever there was pasture.

One day, in the wild country, Moses saw a bush that was on fire. Curiously, it was not burning. As Moses went closer, he heard a voice.

"I am God," it said. "Take off your shoes, for you stand on holy ground.

"Moses – I am choosing you to go back to Egypt. Lead my people to the land I have chosen for them: the land of Canaan, where they can live as my people."

PLAGUES IN EGYPT

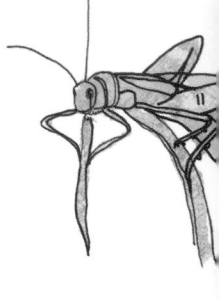

How does one man get a king of Egypt to change his mind? Moses was worried about how he could do as God had asked, and lead his people to freedom.
Then his own brother Aaron came to stand by him in his quest. More than that, God was with him.
So Moses went to the king and asked him to let the Israelite slaves go free.
The king said no.
"If you defy God, disasters will befall Egypt," warned Moses.
Still the king said no.
There followed one disaster after another – plagues of frogs, clouds of gnats, disease, darkness, swarms of locusts...

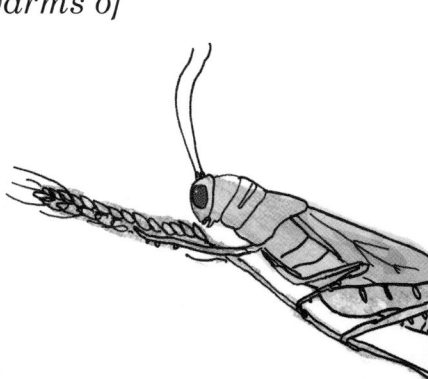

Moses gave
his people warning: "On the
night I say, you must kill a lamb and
mark your door with its blood. The angel
of death will pass over your houses, but in the
homes of the Egyptians, the firstborn will die."
And so it was. The king knew he was beaten.
"Just go!" he ordered.
The people hurried to escape their slavery.
The story of that night, when God rescued his
people, would be told and retold, year after year,
at a festival known as Passover.

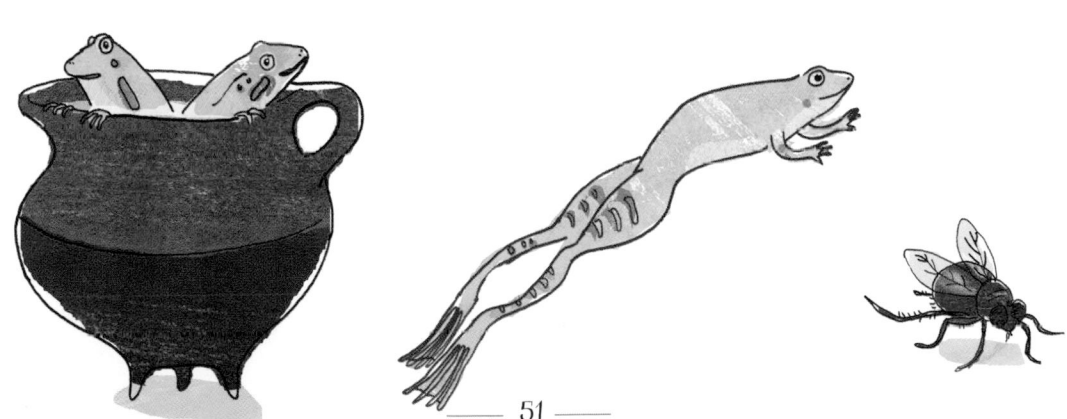

CROSSING THE SEA

Moses took his stick and marched determinedly as he led his people out of Egypt.

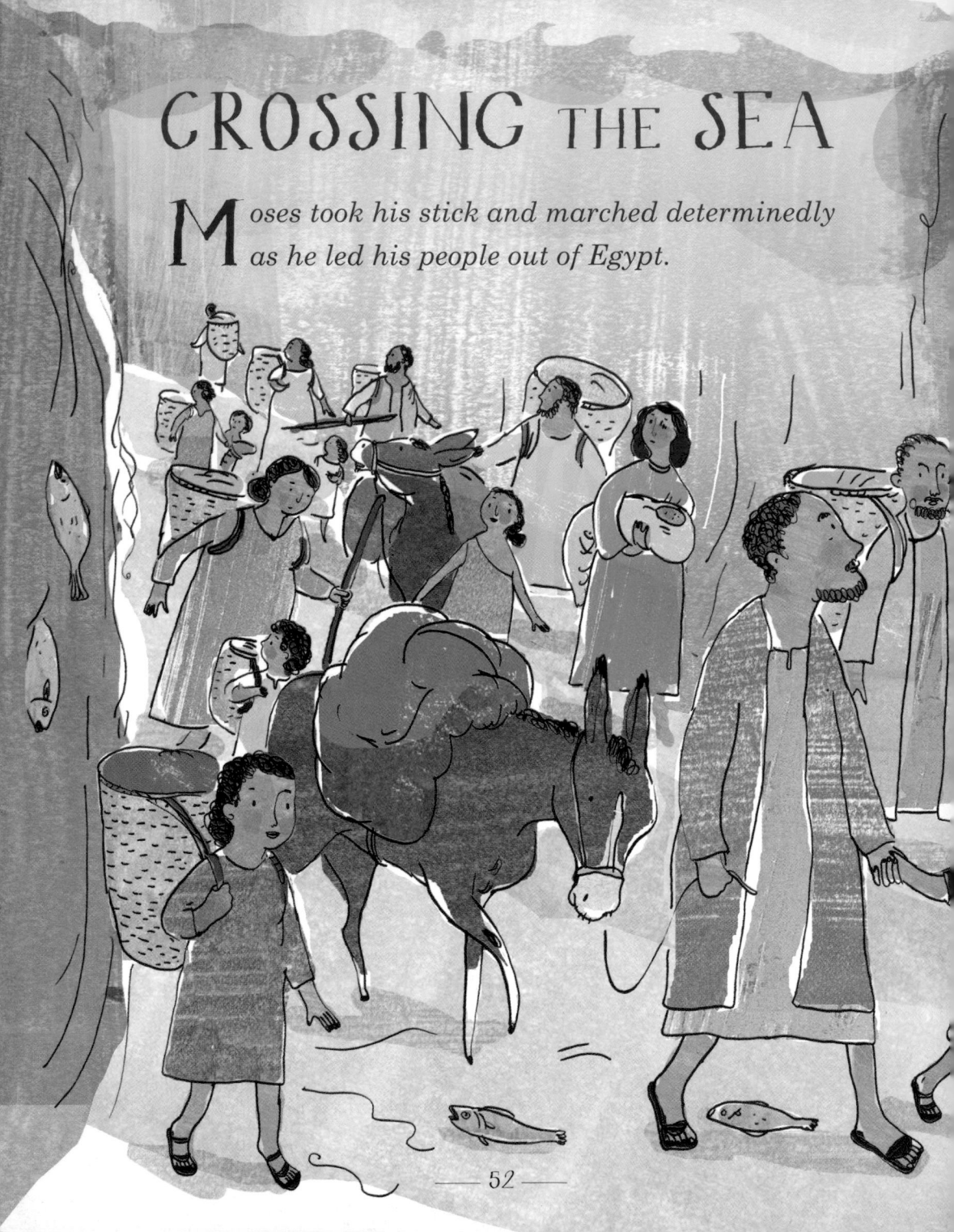

They had just reached the marshy land by the Red Sea when they heard a rumbling. They turned to see what was the cause. Oh, disaster! The king had changed his mind and had sent his chariot regiment to bring his slaves back.

Slowly, boldly, Moses lifted his stick. To everyone's astonishment, the waters parted. God made a path through the sea for his people. They were free:

free from slavery; free to live as God's people.

TEN GREAT COMMANDMENTS

I n between the land of Egypt and the land of Canaan lay the wilderness of Sinai.

For many years, the Israelites lived there as nomads.

On a high mountaintop, God spoke to Moses. "Tell the people of the promise I am making.

"If they live as my people should, then I will be their God.

"Tell them to remember these things:

"I am your God, who set you free. You must worship me alone.

"Do not make idols like other nations do; do not bow down to any false god.

"Do not do evil things and say you are acting in my name.

"Keep the seventh day holy: I set aside the sabbath as a day of rest from the beginning.

"Respect your father and your mother.

"Do not murder.

"Be faithful in marriage.

"Do not steal.

"Do not accuse people of things they have not done.

"Do not want for yourself the things that belong to another.

"If you obey these laws of mine, then I will enable you to make your home in the land of Canaan, and you will prosper there."

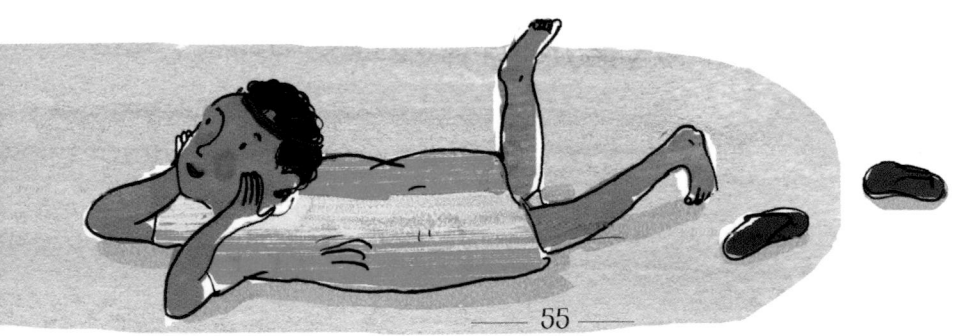

THE GOLDEN CALF

M oses came down the mountain to speak to the people. The great commandments God had given him were engraved on two tablets of stone.

But what did he see? The people had made an idol – a golden calf – and they were singing and dancing around it as if it were their god.

Moses was furious. He smashed the tablets of the Law and ordered that the golden calf be melted down and ground into powder.

Then God saw the people were sorry, and God spoke to Moses. "I am giving you a second set of stone tablets," said God. "Teach my people to obey my laws.

"Remind them that I am a God of love and faithfulness, eager to forgive.

"But evil and wrongdoing will be punished."

God gave Moses instructions for making a fitting place of worship. In its innermost room, there would be a golden box – the ark of the covenant – and inside the box, the tablets of the Law.

THE BATTLE OF JERICHO

When Moses grew old, God chose a young fighter named Joshua to lead the people into Canaan.

God spoke to Joshua: "Be determined and confident, and take care to obey the Law that I gave to Moses.

"Don't be afraid or discouraged, for I will be with you."

So Joshua led the people across the River Jordan into Canaan. Before them stood the city of Jericho.

God told Joshua what to do. Every day for six days Joshua led his fighting men in a procession around the walls. Some priests blew on trumpets while others carried the ark of the covenant high aloft.

On the seventh day they marched seven times around. The priests blew the trumpets. The fighting men gave a great shout.

The walls of Jericho fell down. Joshua took the city.

He encouraged his people to put their trust in God as they claimed the land.

GIDEON'S VICTORY

G ideon had never been a fighter. He was a farmer's son,
better at threshing grain than thrashing enemies.

And his people certainly had enemies. They had forgotten to
stay faithful to God and as a result they fell prey to raiders:
Midianites, from the wild country to the east.

Gideon was scared of them. In fact, he took to threshing his
grain in a wine press, out of sight.

Then a stranger arrived with this mysterious greeting:

"God is with you, brave and mighty man."

Gideon was astonished. Here was one of God's angels,
telling him to become a leader of his people: reminding them
to worship their God faithfully; leading them to victory over
the Midianites.

Somewhat fearfully, Gideon did all that God asked him

to do. He gathered together a fighting force of three hundred warriors.

One night, they surrounded the place where the Midianite raiders had camped. Each had a smouldering torch hidden in a clay jar.

Then, on a signal from Gideon...

CRASH! Three hundred men smashed their jars and brandished their torches, which burst into flame.

PA-DAAH! They blew their trumpets, shattering the quiet of night.

In the camp below, the Midianites panicked. Surely the army lined up against them must be enormous!

They fled in terror. God had given Gideon the victory.

SAMSON

There was one lesson the people of Israel struggled to learn: if they failed to obey their God, then trouble would follow.

And so it was that God allowed the Philistines – the warlike settlers who lived on the western shore – to defeat them. But a husband and wife dedicated their son Samson to God. The sign of their promise was to leave his hair uncut.

And God gave Samson amazing strength. Alone he fought the Philistines, killing their warriors and setting fire to their crops.

Then Samson fell in love with a Philistine beauty named Delilah.

She pestered him to tell her the secret of his strength. Then she betrayed him to her people... who came while he was sleeping and hacked away his long, dark braids. His strength left him.

The Philistines blinded Samson. They locked him in chains and set him to work turning heavy grindstones. Day by day, his hair began to grow.

THE STRONGMAN

One day, the Philistines held a festival in their temple. "Let's get Samson, and have some fun mocking him," they agreed.

In the Philistine temple, Samson reached for two great pillars. He pushed.

The pillars cracked. The temple came crashing down on him... and his people's enemies.

NAOMI AND RUTH

Naomi choked back the tears. Here she was, back in Bethlehem, where she had once lived.

Here she had married. Here she had had two sons. Here life had been good.

Then famine had struck. She and her family had gone to build a new life in Moab. There her husband had died, and later her two sons. Life had turned very bitter.

Her only companion now was a faithful daughter-in-law: Ruth. But how could they make a living? They had no one left to help them.

"It's harvest time," said Ruth. "I'll go gleaning for leftover ears of grain, so we can have food."

The fields where she went to gather grain belonged to a wealthy farmer.

He fell in love with Ruth, and she with him.

They married and had a son, Obed.

Naomi smiled as she held her grandson tight. God had taken care of her. Life was good.

SAMUEL

All too often, the people of Israel forgot about God. Even so, they kept the ark of the covenant in a place of worship at Shiloh.

The priest in charge was Eli, and he was getting old.

His young helper was just a boy: Samuel. It was his job to sleep in the shrine to make sure that the lamps burned safely... and that no one could take the ark.

One night, Samuel awoke. Someone was calling his name.

He ran to Eli. "You called, and so I've come," he said.

"I didn't call," replied Eli. "Please go back to bed."

But the same thing happened a second time, and then a third.

At last Eli understood:

"It must be God who is calling you," he told Samuel.
"If the voice calls again, say, 'Speak: your servant is listening.'"
God did indeed call Samuel's name, and gave a solemn
warning: that Eli's sons were not fit to be priests after him.
Eli bowed his head when Samuel told him God's message.
"God is God," he said sadly. "God will do what seems best."
And so it was that Samuel grew up the next leader of his
people, helping them to remember God and to obey God's
laws.

DAVID AND GOLIATH

The people of Israel did not feel safe in Canaan. From all around they were harassed by enemies. In the end they asked Samuel to choose a warrior king to rescue them.

With God's help, Samuel chose Saul. He led his fighting men to many victories.

Then came the day when he feared he would be defeated. From the ranks of the Philistines came a giant of a man, clad in armour and brandishing fierce weapons.

"Send one of your warriors to fight me!" roared Goliath. "If anyone can beat me, we will declare your side the winner.

"If you can find anyone who'll dare take me on, that is. Ha ha ha ha ha!"

It so happened that a shepherd boy named David was visiting his brothers in the army that day.

"I dare," he told King Saul. "I'm really good with my slingshot and I've killed lions and bears with it.

"If God can help me do that, God can help me defeat Goliath."

The Philistine army watched as their champion strode out to roar his challenge.

The Israelite army watched as David sauntered down to the stream in the valley, picked up five pebbles, and walked on toward Goliath.

"I can beat you because I have put my trust in God," cried David.

He fitted a stone to his sling, whirled it around, and threw.

It struck the giant: he fell down heavily.

The Israelites cheered. They had won! THEY HAD WON!

DAVID'S CITY

When Saul died, David became the new king of Israel. He remained a fearless warrior and led his army to victory over all his people's enemies.

In one daring raid, his fighters captured a hilltop fortress named Jebus.

"Here I will build my royal city," declared David. "Here I will bring the ark of the covenant, as a sign that God's laws are at the heart of the way we live.

"Here I will build a temple to house the ark, and as a place of worship."

DAVID'S SONG

David never forgot that he was once a shepherd boy; that he had once spent his days out in the hills with only his songs and his harp for company.

And he never forgot that through all the years, God had been his shepherd.

He wrote this song:

> Dear God, you are my shepherd
> You give me all I need
> You take me where the grass grows green
> And I can safely feed.
> You take me where the water
> Is calm and cool and clear
> And there I rest and know I'm safe
> For you are always near.

THE WISDOM OF SOLOMON

When David died, his son Solomon became king.

In a dream God spoke to him: "What would you like me to give you?"

"I am very young to be king," replied Solomon, "and I don't really know what to do.

"Give me the wisdom I need to rule your people with justice, and to know the difference between good and evil."

God granted his request. And soon it became very clear that a good king needs great wisdom.

Two women came and asked him to settle their quarrel.

"We each had a baby," said one. "That other woman's baby died in her bed one night. She came and swapped it for mine and she won't give it back."

"Lies!" screamed the second. "It all happened the other way around. This is my baby and I'm keeping him!"

Solomon listened as the two raged at each other. Then...

"Bring a sword," he said calmly. "Cut the living child in two and give each a half."

"Fair enough," agreed one.

"Please no, Your Majesty," wailed the other. "Let her have the baby, but let him live, I beg you."

"He is yours and you will keep him," declared Solomon. "Your love for him proves that you are the real mother."

THE TEMPLE IN JERUSALEM

King Solomon's father David had defeated his people's enemies. Now the kingdom was peaceful and prosperous.

"Here in my father's city of Jerusalem I will build the temple he dreamed of," declared Solomon.

He chose the most skilled workers and the finest materials: stone and pine, cedar wood, olive wood, gleaming bronze, and much fine gold.

When it was done, he called the people together:

"May you always be faithful to your God," he told them, "and may you always obey his laws, as you do today."

74

THE DIVIDED KINGDOM

As the years passed, Solomon grew very wealthy. He also forgot the importance of wisdom, choosing instead to demand that his subjects pay high taxes and do work for no pay so he could live in luxury with his hundreds of wives.

When he died, the people who lived far to the north rebelled. "We will have a king whom we choose," they declared. Their kingdom was known as Israel.

Only the people who lived in the region close to Jerusalem stayed loyal to Solomon's son. Their kingdom was known as Judah.

AHAB AND ELIJAH

There was once a time in the kingdom of Israel when a man named Ahab became king.

He married a foreign princess named Jezebel and she came to live in his royal city of Samaria.

"I want to worship my god Baal," she told him. "I want you to build a temple for that purpose."

So Ahab did.

Now Elijah was a prophet of the God of Israel. "Because of what you have done, there will be no rain for three years," he warned the king. Then, knowing the king would be angry, he went into hiding, drinking from a stream and trusting that ravens would bring him food.

When the three years were over, God told Elijah to go back to King Ahab.

"I challenge Jezebel's prophets to a contest," Elijah said, and he summoned them to Mount Carmel.

"We will offer a sacrifice on a blazing fire. Only this is the test: Jezebel's prophets must ask Baal to light the firewood. I will appeal only to the God of Israel."

The contest began. The firewood was piled high. The prophets of Baal shouted prayers and danced in a frenzy... but nothing happened.

Then Elijah had water poured all over
the wood and said a prayer.

At once fire blazed down from heaven. Elijah had shown
God's power.

And then it began to rain.

NABOTH'S VINEYARD

Near King Ahab's palace in Jezreel was a vineyard. It belonged to a man named Naboth.

"I'd like to buy it," Ahab told him. "It will make a fine vegetable patch. I'll pay good money."

"It's not for sale," replied Naboth.

Ahab went home in a sulk. "What's the matter?" asked Queen Jezebel, and Ahab explained.

"Don't you worry, dearest," she said. "I'll sort everything."

And she did. Only she did it her way: by accusing Naboth of something he hadn't done and having him put to death. Just like that.

When she got the news that her plan had been successful, she went to Ahab. "It's time to come and claim your new vegetable garden," she whispered.

But while Ahab was planning his rows of beans and onions, the prophet Elijah arrived and told him what had happened to Naboth.

For the first time ever, Ahab was really very sorry.

THE PROPHET ELISHA

T he time came for God to take the prophet Elijah up to heaven.

Elijah chose a young prophet named Elisha to carry on the work he had done, reminding people to obey God's laws.

As they walked along together flaming horses galloped between them, pulling a chariot of fire.

Elijah was taken up to heaven in a whirlwind and never seen again.

Now at this time, Namaan was a general in the Syrian army, and a sworn enemy of Israel. In one raid he had captured an Israelite girl and brought her home to be his wife's servant.

But he also suffered from a dreadful skin disease that no one could cure.

"There is a prophet in my country who could help him," announced the servant girl.

Naaman made arrangements to visit Elisha. But although he made the long journey to his home, Elisha merely sent a servant out with a message:

"Bathe seven times in the River Jordan."

"That's ridiculous and insulting," replied Namaan. "There are better rivers in Syria."

His servants persuaded him to try, given that he had come so far.

So he did. And he was cured.

JEHU'S REBELLION

After King Ahab died, his son Joram became king of Israel. But his mother Jezebel was still the power in the land, and still she had no respect for God.

One day, the prophet Elisha sent his servants to a young army officer named Jehu with a message: that God had chosen him to be the next king of Israel.

Jehu gathered a band of loyal soldiers and set out in his chariot.

He hunted down King Joram and shot him with an arrow. The rebellion against Ahab's wicked family had began.

QUEEN JEZEBEL

"Your Majesty," warned a servant. "Jehu has killed your son the king."

Proud Jezebel put on her make-up and did her hair. Then she went to a window high up in the palace and saw Jehu driving his chariot in the street below.

"Why are you here?" she screamed. Jehu looked up. He saw that servants were standing by her side.

"Throw her down," he shouted at them.

Even as the queen lay dying, Jehu went inside the palace to make himself the new king.

After enjoying a meal, he sent servants to bury Jezebel's body. They found only her skull and the bones of her hands and feet. Dogs had eaten the rest.

ISRAEL DEFEATED

I n the kingdom of Israel, both the people and their rulers
were unfaithful to their God. They broke the laws about
worship, and said prayers to the gods of other nations. They
set their hearts on getting rich and having all the luxuries
money could buy; they didn't care one bit about paying fair
wages or taking care of the poor, as the laws clearly said they
should.

The result was disaster. From the north came the terrifying
army of the Assyrian emperor: Sennacherib. He defeated
Israel and sent its people to live in other lands.

JUDAH ATTACKED

At the time of Israel's defeat, King Hezekiah ruled the kingdom of Judah.

He was determined to worship the God of his people respectfully; he did his best to obey all the laws given in the time of Moses.

Even so, the Assyrian army swept down on his kingdom. The city of Lachish was besieged and captured; Hezekiah offered gold and silver in return for peace.

The emperor Sennacherib laughed when he received the riches. Then he ordered his army to march on Jerusalem.

THE SIEGE
OF JERUSALEM

T he Assyrian army set up camp outside the city of
   Jerusalem: thousands upon thousands of soldiers with
deadly weapons of war.

   But they were in no hurry to attack; they would simply lay
siege until the unfortunates inside the city ran short of food
and water.

   Now there was in Jerusalem a holy man – a prophet named
Isaiah.

   Hezekiah was desperate to hear his advice: what should he
do? What was the best thing to do to defend his people – God's
people?

86

Isaiah's message was full of encouragement:

"Your Assyrian enemies can only win if God allows. As it is, God has chosen to protect Jerusalem. There will not be a siege. No arrow will be fired. Sennacherib will go home."

That night, the angel of death swept through the Assyrian camp. In the morning many thousands of soldiers lay cold and still.

As the holy man had prophesied, Emperor Sennacherib led his army home.

THE PEACEABLE KINGDOM

The Assyrian invasion left the people of Judah in despair. Long ago, King David had led the nation to victory. His triumph had now been swept aside.

"Listen," said the prophet Isaiah. "One day, a new king will be born from the family line of David. God will give him the wisdom to rule his people. He will bring justice to the poor and take care of those in need.

"Those who do evil will get the punishment they deserve.

"In his peaceable kingdom, wolves and sheep will live together; leopards with goats, calves with lion cubs, and little children will take care of them.

"Everyone in the whole wide world will know that God is God."

KING JOSIAH

J osiah was just eight years old when he became king of
Judah. Even though he was so young, he already had
great respect for God's laws and tried to
obey them.

When he was a grown man, he noticed
that the Temple in Jerusalem was
looking quite shabby. He gave orders
that builders be hired to repair it.

While they were at work,
they found an old scroll lying
neglected in a corner. "We'd better
give this to the priest who can
read it," they agreed.

What the priest read was
astonishing: the scroll was a book
of the Law from long ago. As he
read it, he realized that many
of the laws had been completely
forgotten! The people had not been faithful to their covenant
with God.

A message was sent to King Josiah. He acted swiftly:

"From now on, we must worship our God in the proper and respectful way," he said. "First we will set everything in the Temple to rights.

"Then we will celebrate Passover – the festival to recall the night that Moses led our people out of slavery."

It was the first time in hundreds of years that the people had shown such respect for their God and their traditions.

JUDAH DEFEATED

King Nebuchadnezzar of Babylon had ambitions. He wanted to rule a vast empire. He had given orders that his armies defeat the nations all around.

Already he had won many victories. Now he wanted to defeat the kingdom of Judah.

Neither its king nor its people could stop him doing what he liked. He stole all the treasures in Jerusalem. He took as his prisoners all those whom he could usefully set to work.

He left behind the poor people and a young king, Zedekiah, who was to rule on his behalf.

As the years went by, Zedekiah grew bold. "I'm not going to take my orders from Babylon," he decided. "It's time to rebel."

King Nebuchadnezzar was furious. He ordered his army to attack Jerusalem and destroy it.

The Temple was torn down. Its remaining treasures were looted.

And what about the ark of the covenant – the symbol of God's promise to be with his people?

No one knew. It had gone, never to be seen again.

THE FIERY FURNACE

King Nebuchadnezzar wanted complete obedience from everyone in his empire.

One day, he summoned all his officials from far and wide to Babylon.

On the plain outside the city stood a huge golden statue. A herald called his message:

"People of all nations, races, and languages. In a moment, the musicians will play. When you hear the music, you must bow down – by order of King Nebuchadnezzar."

Now among the people who had been brought to Babylon from Judah were three young men: Shadrach, Meshach, and Abednego.

They were determined to worship their God alone and they simply refused to bow down.

"Make the fiery furnace as hot as it can be," screamed Nebuchadnezzar. "Throw them in."

The three men were tied up and hurled into the flames.

But when the king went to look, he saw something amazing.

They were not bound any more; instead, they were walking around… and with them was an angel.

Nebuchadnezzar was terrified.

"Pull those men out of the flames at once!" he commanded. "Clearly their God is great and mighty. No other god can rescue like this."

BY THE RIVERS

"We are far from home."

The people of Judah who lived in Babylon awoke every day with this great sadness in their hearts.

They began to meet every week, on the sabbath day of rest, down by the rivers of Babylon. It was a time to remember their faith, their laws, and their traditions.

"Oh look! It's the people from Judah – the Jews," said passers-by. "Do tell us about your home country. Perhaps you could sing us one of your songs!"

The Jews shook their heads. They were too sad to sing.

A prophet named Ezekiel brought them some hope:

OF BABYLON

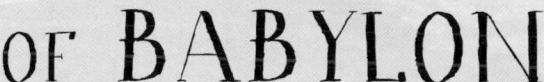

"God says this: 'Just as a good shepherd gathers together his flock, I will gather my people and lead them home.

"'I will look for those that are lost, bring back those that wander off, bandage those that are hurt, and heal those that are sick.

"'I will bring them to a place of peace and safety.

"'You, my sheep, the flock that I feed, are my people, and I am your God.'"

THE WRITING ON THE WALL

King Belshazzar was as godless as his father, Nebuchadnezzar.

One night, he threw a huge banquet. It turned into a riotous drinking party.

Suddenly, terrifyingly, a mysterious human hand appeared to the revellers. It began writing on the wall.

"Why has this happened? What do the words mean?" Belshazzar cried.

The queen mother offered her advice. "Your father knew of no better advisor than one of the Jews: a man named Daniel. He may be able to help."

Daniel was summoned without delay. His message was sombre.

"Your days are numbered, you lightweight!" he warned the king. "Your kingdom will be divided among others."

That night, Darius the Mede seized the throne.

IN THE COURT OF KING DARIUS

The new king, Darius, needed to find the best people to help govern his kingdom. He then needed to find the very best people to manage the governors. He discovered that the wisest and most trustworthy of these was Daniel, and he put him in charge.

That left others furious with jealousy.

"Let's get rid of Daniel," they agreed.

"It won't be easy – he's always so reliable and honest in everything he does!"

"But he is a Jew and he's very loyal to his faith. Let's try and use that loyalty against him."

Together, three conspirators made a plan.

THE PLOT AGAINST DANIEL

King Darius liked to be treated with respect. He was rather pleased when three officials came and bowed low in front of him.

"O King, may you live for ever," they began. "All of the officials in your empire are of one mind.

"You should make a law that for thirty days no one should appeal for anything from any human or any god except you, great king, Your Majesty.

"And," they added, "the law should say that anyone who disobeys will be thrown into a pit of lions."

"What a good idea," agreed Darius. "It will be a law of the Medes and Persians, and such a law cannot be changed."

The three conspirators went to spy on Daniel. They were delighted at what they saw. He was at his window, looking in the direction of Jerusalem, saying prayers to his God.

They went and told the king. He was not pleased.

"The law isn't to catch Daniel," he snapped.
"I can trust him to stay loyal."

"But the law of the Medes and Persians cannot be changed,"
wheedled the conspirators. "He must be thrown to the lions."

Darius was trapped. And very soon, so was Daniel. In a pit
of lions.

IN THE LIONS' DEN

King Darius spent a sleepless night.

His best and most trusted official had been Daniel.

And right now, even as he paced around the palace, the lions were pacing around Daniel.

And almost certainly pouncing on him. And sinking their teeth into him. And crunching his bones... It was all so dreadful.

As soon as it was light, Darius hurried to the lion pit.

"Daniel," he called nervously. He wasn't expecting a reply.

"Hello!" called Daniel. "I mean, may Your Majesty live for ever.

"You find me alive and well. God sent an angel to keep the lions from eating me.

"God knows I've done nothing wrong."

King Darius was overcome with emotion. "Pull that man out of danger at once," he ordered.

"Then go and get the wretches who tried to have him killed, and throw them in the pit. The lions will get a very big dinner today.

"And now I will issue a proclamation: Daniel's God is a living god, the God who will rule for ever."

KING XERXES
MUST BE OBEYED

From his palace in the Persian city of Susa, King Xerxes ruled a great empire.

He expected everyone to obey him without question.

But on one occasion, his wife, Queen Vashti, refused to come to his summons.

Furious, he decided to banish her and choose a new queen – on the basis of who was the most beautiful young woman in his empire.

A search was made, and the choice went to Esther.

Uncle Mordecai, who had raised the young orphan, was anxious about what lay ahead.

"Be careful in the palace," he warned his niece. "Don't tell them *you're Jewish. Not many people like the Jews."*

Even so, Esther became queen, while Mordecai got a job in the government. When he heard of a plot to kill the king, he passed a message to Esther. She in turn told the king and the conspirators were arrested.

Xerxes was naturally grateful. "Make a note of Mordecai's loyal deed," he told a servant. "Put it on record."

So the deed was recorded. And promptly forgotten.

As time went by, King Xerxes chose a man named Haman to be his chief advisor. It just so happened he was also enemy-in-chief of the Jews. Right away he persuaded the king to name the day on which they should be massacred.

QUEEN ESTHER

Queen Esther put on her finery. It was strictly forbidden to go to the king without being summoned, but Mordecai had told her of the plot against her people, the Jews. Fearful and determined, she went to the throne room.

Esther did look lovely, and the king was in a good mood. "Queen Esther!" he cried. "What is it you want?"

"I'd like you and Haman to come to dinner," she said, and the king agreed. The banquet was such a success that another was planned for the following evening.

As Haman headed home, he saw Mordecai.

"I hate that Jew," he muttered. "I'll have a gallows built, and I'll hang him."

Little did he know that King Xerxes was just then rediscovering the story of how Mordecai had once saved his life.

In the morning, Xerxes gave Haman a special task.

"I want you to organize a reward for a great man," he said. And Haman had to conduct a parade of thanks for the Jew he planned to hang.

Even so, the evening's banquet with the king and queen began to cheer him up.

Then, when the lavish dinner was over, King Xerxes
asked Esther to say what she wanted.

"Please allow me and my people to live," she declared.
"Our enemy is that evil man there!"

Xerxes ordered that Haman be hanged on the very
gallows he had built for Mordecai, and that the Jews be
allowed to defend themselves from all their enemies.

In this way, Queen Esther saved her people.

DRY BONES

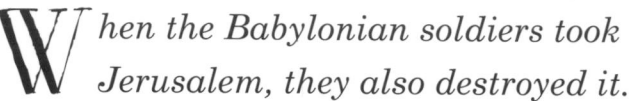

W hen the Babylonian soldiers took Jerusalem, they also destroyed it.

Many of the defeated Jews who were taken to live in faraway Babylon wept when they remembered the disaster.

"Listen," said the prophet named Ezekiel. "I dreamed God showed me a valley full of dry human bones.

"As I watched, I heard a rattling. The bones joined up into skeletons and flesh grew over them…

"Then God spoke to me: 'Tell the wind to blow life into these bodies.'

"I did so… and the bodies came to life.

"And I am sure that this is the meaning of my dream: though the nation seems dead, God will give it new life."

CELEBRATION

Years went by, and Persians defeated the Babylonians. They gave permission for the Jews to go back to their homeland.

So it was that a band of Jews set out for the ruins of Jerusalem. Slowly, carefully, they rebuilt the Temple.

"Listen to what God has told me," declared a prophet named Haggai.

"'When Moses led the nation out of Egypt, I promised that I would always be with you. I am still with you, so do not be afraid.'"

The words gave the people the hope they needed. They celebrated the festival of Passover beside their new Temple: to remember God's blessing in days of old, and in their own day.

109

EZRA

Many years later, a priest named Ezra left Babylon for Jerusalem.

Ezra was a scholar. He had spent long years studying God's ancient laws. He always tried to obey them faithfully, and he was eager to make sure that his people understood them.

But what did he find in Jerusalem? Jews who seemed to have forgotten their own traditions.

"Our people should live differently from other people," he cried, "yet some of you have married foreign wives! How can you raise good Jewish families?"

And he ordered the people to live separately from foreigners – even their own wives!

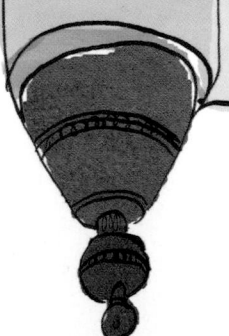

NEHEMIAH

Around this time lived a Jew named Nehemiah. He worked as butler to the Persian emperor Artaxerxes.

One day, as he was serving the wine, Artaxerxes asked him a surprising question.

"You're looking very sad today. That's not like you at all! What's the matter?"

Nehemiah was startled. He said a quick prayer of "Help!" before answering.

"I'm thinking of my homeland," he said. "I hear that the once great city of Jerusalem is still not rebuilt. I would love to go and help."

"Then you shall," replied the emperor. "I will give you all the help you need."

111

THE WALLS

Nehemiah made the long journey to Jerusalem. Under cover of darkness, he rode around the city. His donkey picked its way among the rubble of the ruined walls. The whole place was a shambles.

"I shall put myself in charge of the rebuilding," Nehemiah said to himself. "I want the Jews to have a city they can be proud of."

Nehemiah was a great organizer. Soon his plans were underway.

Some of the foreigners who lived nearby were scornful. "What terrible workmanship!" they laughed. "Call this thing a wall? A fox could knock it down!"

The mocking was bad enough, but there was worse to come: the foreigners made a plan to come and destroy the new walls.

# of JERUSALEM

"We will defend ourselves," announced Nehemiah. "Some of us must stand guard while the others work. We won't let ourselves be bullied."

At last the work was done.

Ezra came and read the Law to all the people of Jerusalem.

It reminded them to celebrate the festival of Shelters, and the time when the people had lived as wanderers in the wilderness after they had escaped from Egypt.

It was also a reminder of the time after that, when God had helped them make their home in Canaan – just as they were now making their home in Jerusalem.

THE STORY OF JONAH

The Jews were proud of the newly rebuilt Jerusalem. How could they not be? They had been cruelly treated by other nations. Now they wanted to be free to follow their own traditions.

But did God really not like any other nations, as Ezra hinted? The story of Jonah provided a surprise.

Long ago, when the Assyrians ruled the world from the city of Nineveh, there lived a prophet named Jonah.

"I have a special mission for you," said God one day. "Go to Nineveh and warn the people not to be so wicked."

Jonah was annoyed. He didn't want to go to where his

people's enemies lived!

So he did not take the road north to Nineveh.

Instead, he took the road to the port of Joppa. He found a boat that was soon to sail far, far away. He paid his fare and got on board.

The sailors untied the boat from its mooring.

"Hooray!" said Jonah to himself. "I'm going as far from Nineveh as anyone can go. Let them live as wickedly as they like – and die that way too!"

115

DOWN IN THE DEEP

The boat that carried Jonah sailed far out to sea. Jonah settled down below decks to sleep.

Then, in the night, God sent a storm. The wind howled. The waves crashed.

"Some god wants to drown us!" cried the sailors. "Who has made their god angry?"

In fear for their lives, the sailors cast lots to find the culprit.

It was Jonah.

"I confess!" wailed Jonah. "I'm running away from a mission God gave me. Throw me into the sea, and save yourselves."

The sailors were at first afraid to do so, but the storm grew worse.

"Sorry!" they cried, as they heaved Jonah into the sea.

Down, down, down he went. In the murky depths, a huge fish swallowed him up.

It seemed like the end, but, in that stinking belly, Jonah could breathe.

At last he came to his senses.

"I'm sorry, God," he said. "Please rescue me, and I will do as you ask."

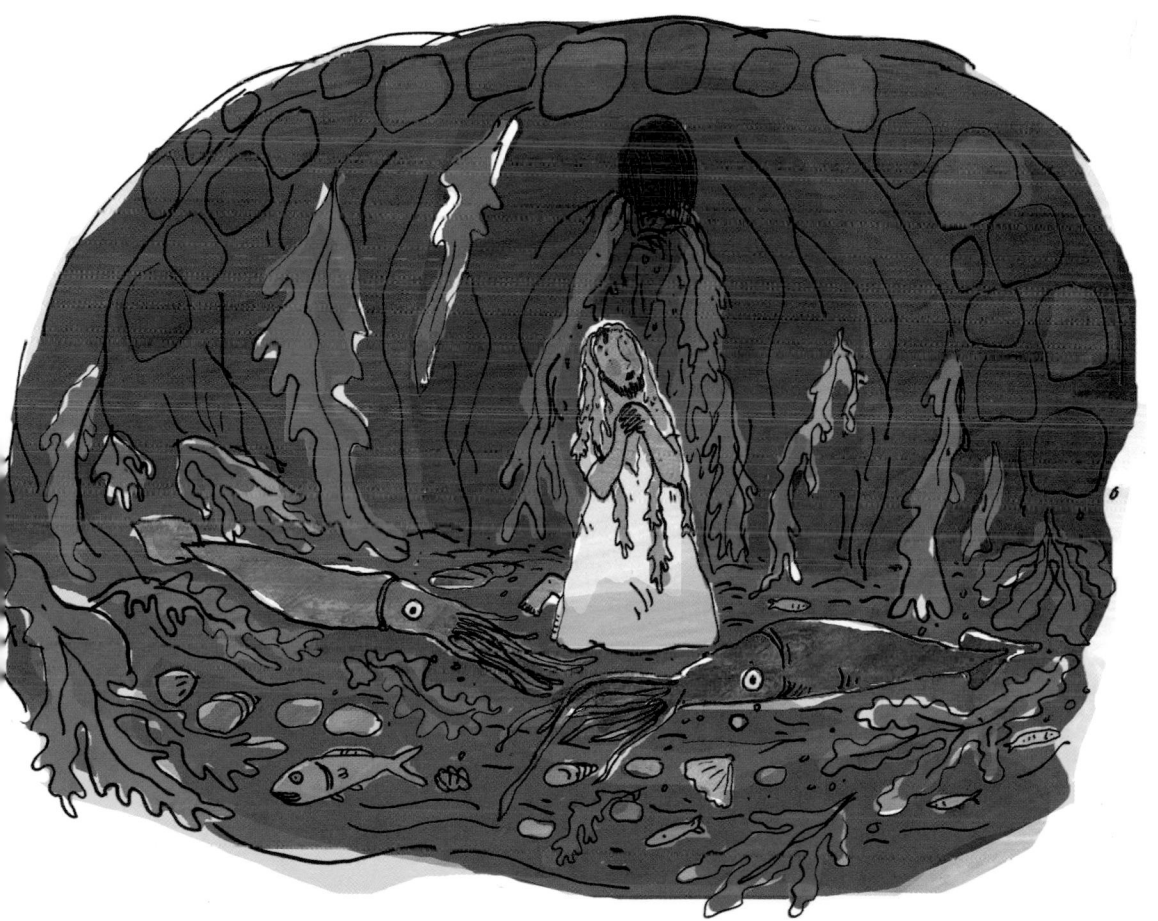

IN NINEVEH

God really did want Jonah to go to Nineveh; and when the great fish heaved Jonah up onto a beach, the prophet hurried to the city of his enemies.

"Listen up!" he cried. "God is angry at your wickedness. Change your ways, or God will destroy the city."

The people listened. The king listened. The children listened. Everyone listened – and then they changed their ways.

Jonah went a little way off to watch what would happen. Would God punish the wicked people of Nineveh?

God did not.

Jonah was furious. He built himself
a little shelter and sulked. "I knew you'd
forgive them," he muttered to God.

Then the sun rose. The day grew hot.
"And now I'm dying in the heat," complained
Jonah.

God caused a plant to grow. Its leaves gave cool
shade, and Jonah was pleased.

Then God sent a worm to eat the stalk. The plant wilted.
"Oh no!" wailed Jonah. "My poor, dear, lovely plant."

God was listening. "You care a lot about
a plant," said God. "Now perhaps you
understand why I care about Nineveh
– its people, its children, and all
its animals."

THE NEW TESTAMENT

W hen the Jews rebuilt their city of Jerusalem, it seemed as if they might be able to live in peace and freedom. That was not to be. From the west came the Greek armies, defeating the Persians and establishing a new empire. The Greeks wanted everyone to respect their traditions, and they even put statues of their own gods in the Jewish Temple.

The Jews were dismayed. In the end, they rebelled and demanded to be allowed to follow their own traditions.

So began an uneasy time: the Jews still had to respect foreign rulers, but they were allowed to follow their own traditions. Every week, each community would gather in the synagogue to learn about their faith.

Then the Romans came with their armies and made the land of the Jews part of their empire.

"Will we ever be free?" the Jews wondered. "Did not our prophets say that God would send a king like David to be our saviour? If only!"

MARY AND THE ANGEL

Nazareth was just a quiet little town in Galilee, surround by fields and pastures. It was home to a young woman named Mary, who was looking forward to getting married.

One day in spring, the angel Gabriel came and greeted her. Mary was astonished.

"Don't be afraid!" said the angel. "God has chosen you to be the mother of his son. You will name him 'Jesus'. He will become known as the Son of God, the king of an everlasting kingdom."

Mary shook her head. "I can't be a mother," she said. "I'm not yet married."

"God can make this happen," said the angel quietly.

Mary's reply was simple; "I will do what God wants," she said.

JOSEPH
LEADS THE WAY

J oseph looked up from his workbench and sighed. His bride-to-be, Mary, was expecting someone else's baby.

"I'll have to cancel everything," he said to himself. "I'm so sad."

Then, in a dream, an angel spoke to him.

"Joseph: the right thing to do is to marry Mary. Her child is God's child.

"He will show people the good and right way to live."

Joseph woke up feeling much happier. He went to find Mary.

"You know about the order from the Roman emperor," he said, "that everyone must go to their home town and put their names on a great long list."

"Oh yes," replied Mary. "Everyone on that list is going to get a big tax bill."

"Well, yes," said Joseph. "But listen: my family can trace its roots back to King David, so my home town is Bethlehem. Let's go together to register as taxpayers – for we are going to be husband and wife."

The journey took several days. When they arrived, Bethlehem was crowded.

The only place they could find to stay was a stable. There, in the night, Mary's baby was born.

SHEPHERDS AND ANGELS

Out on the hillside near Bethlehem, some shepherds were watching over their sheep: keeping them safe in the fold, away from wild animals and wicked thieves.

They felt someone watching them and turned.

It was an angel!

"Don't be afraid," said the angel. "I bring the very best of news. Tonight, in Bethlehem, a special baby has been born. He is God's promised king – the Christ, the messiah.

"You should go and find him: he is snugly wrapped in swaddling clothes and lying in a manger."

Suddenly, the dark of night burst into brightness. Thousands of dazzling angels danced and sang, "Glory to God in highest heaven, and peace on earth."

It seemed to the shepherds that they were looking into heaven itself.

THE BABY IN THE MANGER

The angels vanished as suddenly as they had appeared. The shepherds looked at one another. Was the angel's message true? Was there really a newborn baby in Bethlehem?

"Let's make the sheep safe, and go and see," they agreed.

They hurried off to Bethlehem's dark streets. In a shabby stable, where an ox munched and a donkey stamped and shuffled, they found Joseph and Mary and little baby Jesus.

Everything was just as the angel had said.

Mary smiled as the shepherds told her about the angels and what they had said.

She knew the stories of her faith. She knew about the promise to her people that one day God would send a king like David.

And here, in the very town where king David had been born, was her own child:

God's own Son, God's promised king.

THE WISE MEN

In a land far to the east, some wise and learned men were looking at the night sky.

"It most certainly IS a new star up in the sky," they agreed. "It must be a special sign that a new king has been born.

"And see where it points: to the land of the Jews."

"We should go and bow down to His Majesty."

They set out on a long journey. When they reached Jerusalem, they began asking about a newborn king.

AND THE STAR

King Herod, who ruled the Jewish nation on behalf of the Roman emperor, was troubled at the news. He asked his own wise men for their advice.

"The Jewish prophets speak of a messiah," they said. "Our people believe that one day God will send a king like David to save our people from all their woes.

"Like David himself, he will be born in Bethlehem."

King Herod smiled grimly. "Bring those stargazers to me," he said.

In a secret meeting, Herod sent the wise men to Bethlehem with one instruction. "Find the king," he said, "and then come and tell me where he is. I too will go and worship him."

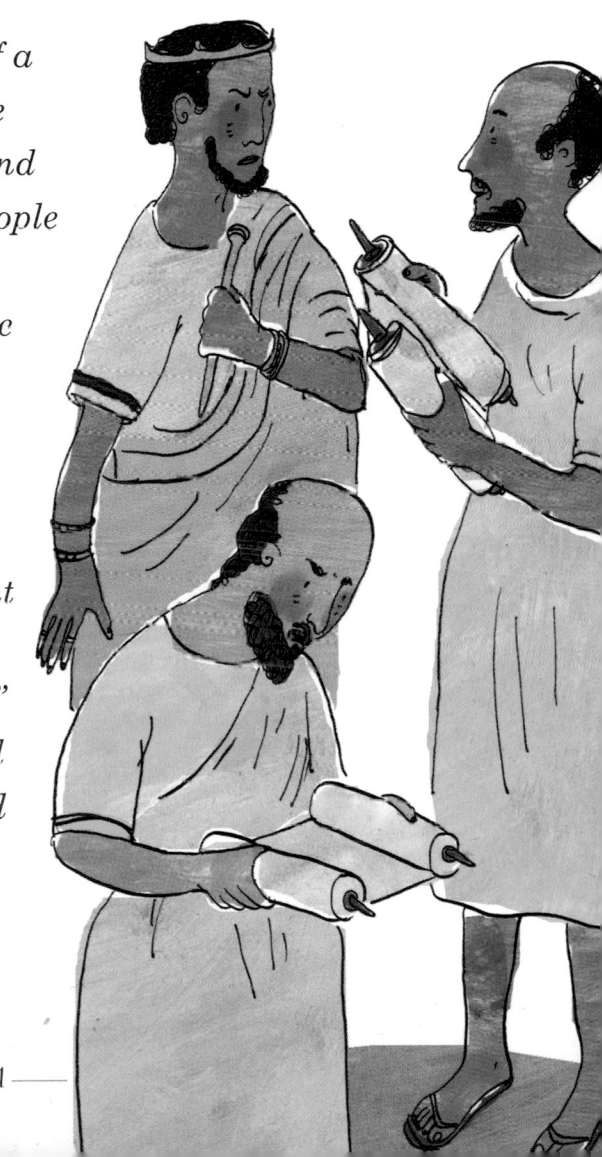

THREE GIFTS

The wise men set out from Jerusalem along the Bethlehem road.

The star that had led them so far shone its light on their way.

Then it stopped, bathing one house in Bethlehem with its mysterious light.

Inside the men found Mary and Jesus.

They brought out rich gifts: gold, frankincense, and myrrh.

In the night, the wise men each had a dream. It warned them that Herod planned to harm the child.

"We will go home by a different road," they agreed.

Not long after, Joseph had a dream in which an angel appeared to him.

"Hurry – take the child and his mother and go to Egypt.

"Stay there until I tell you it is safe."

Joseph did as the angel said. In the dark of night, the little family made their escape.

JESUS GROWS UP

When Mary and Joseph went home to Nazareth, everyone was eager to see their young son. Jesus grew up with the other children there. Like the other boys, he went to school. He learned about his Jewish faith and traditions; he learned to read the holy books of his people. On the sabbath he went to worship God in the synagogue.

Every year, Mary and Joseph went to Jerusalem, to celebrate the Passover festival at the Temple there.

When Jesus was twelve – and so almost grown up – he went too, along with a crowd of pilgrims from Nazareth.

The festival lasted several days, and the crowd from Nazareth felt like one big family.

When they set off for home, Mary only tutted mildly not to see Jesus.

"A young lad will want to be at the front of the group, I suppose," said Joseph.

But when evening came, and the group were setting up camp, Jesus was not there. Not at all. No one had seen him all day. Where could he be?

WHERE IS JESUS?

Mary and Joseph were beside themselves with worry. Where was Jesus? They hurried back along the road to Jerusalem, hoping at any moment to find him straggling along.

But Jesus wasn't out on the road. Mary and Joseph hurried the long miles and saw no sign of him; nor did they find anyone who had seen a young lad on his own.

So perhaps he was still in Jerusalem? For three days Mary and Joseph searched: in the places they had stayed, at the markets where they had shopped, in the streets where they had wandered.

Then, at last, they found Jesus: in the colonnade of the Temple, talking with the rabbis who had studied the Jewish faith and taught it to others.

Jesus was explaining what he believed about his faith and his God, and the rabbis were looking impressed.

Mary was not. She marched over: "What are you doing here?" she cried. "Why did you stay here and leave us so upset?"

"Didn't you know I'd be here?" said Jesus, sounding surprised. "This Temple is my Father's house."

Even so, he said his goodbyes and returned to Nazareth. There he grew up a good and obedient son.

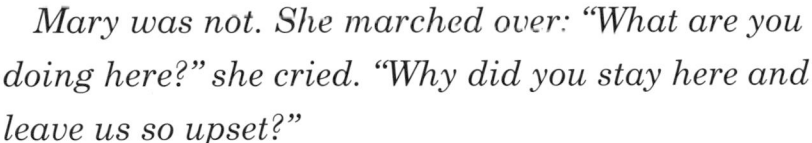

COUSIN JOHN

Jesus had a cousin named John, who was just a little bit older than him.

John's parents, Zechariah and Elizabeth, absolutely doted on him.

"They were not young when they had him," Mary explained to Jesus. "They thought they were getting too old to have children. Then, one day, when Uncle Zechariah was on duty at the Temple, something amazing happened.

"He was in the innermost room – the Holy of Holies, where they burn incense – when he saw an angel. It was the angel who said that he and Elizabeth would have a son, someone who would grow up wise and holy and thoughtful.

"When the baby was born, Zechariah came over all poetic and even said the child would grow up to be a prophet."

Jesus smiled at his mother. "He's made a start on that now, hasn't he?" said Jesus.

"Yes," said Mary, rather hesitantly. "I'm not sure what Elizabeth thinks about it all: living in the desert, dressed up in a ragged old cloak, and foraging for his food."

She shook her head. Whatever was John up to? Then again, what might her own son become?

JOHN THE BAPTIST

*J*esus' cousin John did look rather unkempt, and his preaching was rather forceful – but he did get quite a following.

All kinds of people went out of their way to go and listen to him.

He rebuked people for being sinful, selfish, and unjust. They took his warning seriously.

He offered to baptize people in the River Jordan as a sign they were going to turn their lives around.

Many agreed.

Then, one day, Jesus arrived and asked to be baptized.

"You don't need to do that," replied John. "You haven't done any wrong."

Jesus insisted. John lowered his cousin for a moment under the flowing water of the Jordan. As he lifted him up, God's Holy Spirit fluttered down from heaven in the form of a dove. A voice spoke from heaven: "You are my own dear Son. I am pleased with you."

TEMPTATION

After he was baptized, Jesus went out alone into the wilderness.

There he stayed for forty days, thinking of his new calling... to be a preacher.

While he was there, the Devil came and whispered.

"You must be feeling hungry. If you are God's Son, you could order this stone to turn into bread."

Jesus shook his head. "I've read the holy books, the Scriptures," he said. "They say that people cannot live on bread alone."

Time passed, and the Devil came whispering again.

IN THE WILDERNESS

"Picture, if you will, all the kingdoms of the world. If you worship me, I will give them to you."

"I will not do that," replied Jesus. "The Scriptures say this: 'Worship God alone.'"

A third time the Devil came: "Now imagine yourself on the highest point of the Temple. You throw yourself down – and yet you land unharmed. God will send his angels to make sure you are not in the least bit hurt."

"I will not do that," replied Jesus. "The Scriptures say this: 'Do not put God to the test.'"

After that, the Devil gave up. Jesus was sure of what he had to do, and he would not be tempted to give up.

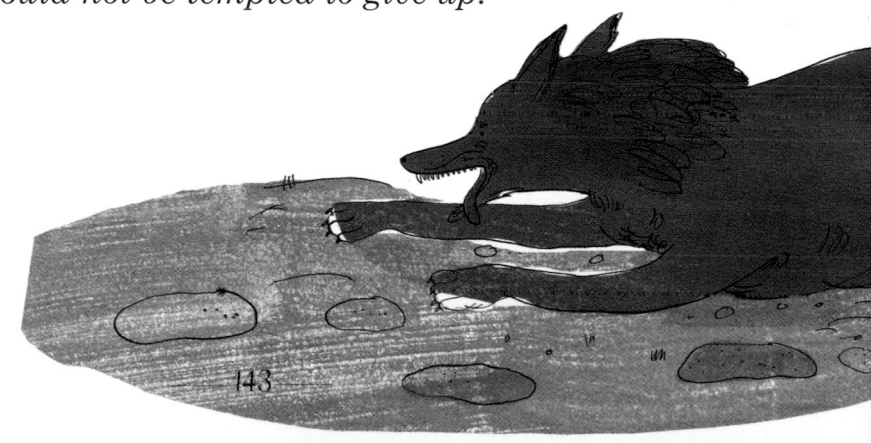

REJECTED

*J*esus went back to Galilee and became a preacher. He went from place to place, preaching in the synagogues where communities gathered for worship.

What he had to say seemed new and interesting. He received lots of invitations to come and speak.

One day, Jesus went to his home synagogue in Nazareth. He was invited to read from the Scriptures. The reading for the day was from the book of the prophet Isaiah.

"The Spirit of the Lord is upon me," he read, "because he has chosen me to bring good news to the poor."

As he finished reading the passage he added, "Today, those words have come true."

The people of Nazareth were puzzled. "Isn't this Joseph's son?" they whispered among themselves.

"You may have heard of wonderful things I've been doing in Capernaum," Jesus went on, "but I won't be able to do anything here. A prophet is never welcome in their own town."

At that, the people were enraged. "A prophet, are you?" they cried. "You arrogant scoundrel."

An angry mob gathered around him. They meant to harm him... but somehow Jesus slipped through the crowd and went on his way.

IN CAPERNAUM

Jesus left Nazareth for the fishing village of Capernaum, on the shores of Lake Galilee.

When the sabbath came, Jesus gave a talk at the synagogue. Most listened carefully. Just one man started shouting and screaming.

"Have you come to destroy us? I know who you are – you're God's chosen messenger, aren't you?"

Jesus spoke calmly, as if to the man's inner demons: "Be quiet," he said, "and leave that man alone."

At once, the man was healed.

When synagogue was over, Jesus spent the day quietly with one of his friends – a fisherman named Simon. They arrived back from synagogue to find Simon's mother-in-law suffering from a high fever. With just a word, Jesus healed her, and she was able to get up and welcome them as she would have wanted.

But news of the first healing spread. As the sun set, marking the end of the sabbath, crowds gathered outside the house where Jesus was. They brought with them those who were ill. One by one, with a simple touch, Jesus healed them all.

JESUS AND THE FISHERMEN

O ne day, when Jesus was down by the shore of Lake Galilee, a large crowd gathered to listen to him. As the people pressed closer, Jesus noticed his friend Simon on the beach along with other fishermen.

"Can I please sit in your boat, and you float it a little way off shore?" he asked. "That way, everyone will be able to see me." Simon agreed cheerfully.

All day long, Jesus spoke to the people about something he called God's kingdom – a new way of living, as friends of God. Everyone listened eagerly.

Later, when the crowds were leaving, Jesus told the fishermen to push their boats out for a catch.

"It's not worth it," said Simon. "We fished all last night and got nothing."

Jesus insisted. No sooner had the fisherman let down their nets than they were full of fish. It felt weird – a miracle, perhaps.

"Don't be afraid," said Jesus. "Now leave your nets, and come and join me as we gather people into God's kingdom."

The fishermen who came were Simon with his brother Andrew, and James with his brother John.

THE HOLE
IN THE ROOF

Ɲews about Jesus and his preaching kept spreading. But was his teaching true? Religious experts including rabbis and Pharisees wanted to know.

One day, a great many of them met Jesus in a house in Galilee. There was simply no room for anyone else.

Then four men came along. They had a friend who couldn't walk, and they had carried him on his sleeping mat, hoping that Jesus would heal him.

They made a new plan: they carried their friend up the outside staircase onto the flat roof. They scrabbled away the plaster to make a hole, and then they lowered their friend down in front of Jesus.

"Your sins are forgiven, my friend," exclaimed Jesus.

The religious experts began muttering. "Jesus can't say that! Only God can forgive sins."

Jesus looked at them. "I can say that and mean it," he said, "and I'll show you by saying something much more difficult."

He turned to the man. "Get up, my friend," he said. "Pick up that mat, and walk home."

At once the man who had been crippled was healed.

JESUS AND THE

O ne day, when Jesus was in a market square, he saw a tax collector named Matthew sitting in his booth.

Now, the Jewish people thought of their tax collectors as villains.

For one thing, they were working for the Romans – the foreign superpower that ruled the land.

For another, most of them lied about how much the Romans wanted. They overcharged people so they could keep the extra themselves.

Jesus went to Matthew and said this: "Follow me."

Matthew left his tax booth and became a devoted follower.

TAX COLLECTOR

One of the first things he did was to invite Jesus to a feast at his house so he could meet all his tax collector friends.

"Look at him," sneered the religious experts. "What kind of preacher is friends with scum like that?"

Jesus' reply was brief. "People who are well don't need a doctor," he said, "but the sick do. So my message is not for respectable people, but for the outcasts."

RULES, RULES

One sabbath day, Jesus was walking through a field of grain. The crop was nearly ready, and Jesus' friends were hungry. They began to pick the seed heads so they could eat the grain.

Some Pharisees were watching.

"Why are you breaking the Law?" they asked Jesus. "You know what it says: no one is to work on the sabbath."

"Don't you know the stories of our great King David?" replied Jesus. "He once gave his followers bread even though it had been offered to God because they were hungry.

"The rules about the sabbath are there to help people, not make slaves of them."

Not long after, Jesus was preaching in a synagogue on a sabbath day. He saw a man whose arm was paralysed. Some rabbis were watching: would Jesus break the sabbath and heal him?

Jesus called the man to the front. "What does our Law allow us to do on the Sabbath?" he asked the rabbis. "To help, or to harm?"

Then he turned to the man, and healed him.

TWELVE DISCIPLES

*A*ll over the country, people were eager to hear Jesus' message: about God's kingdom of love and forgiveness.

It just wasn't possible for Jesus to go everywhere and preach to everyone.

Already he had a band of chosen followers. Now he needed more.

Jesus spent a whole night praying before he made his choice:

There was Simon, whom he regarded as his rock. In fact, he nicknamed him "Peter", because the word means "rock".

Then there was Simon's brother Andrew, James and John, Philip and Bartholomew, Matthew and Thomas, and another James.

There was another Simon too: the second one had been a freedom fighter. It was almost a surprise that Jesus chose him; Jesus didn't think violence was the right way to change things.

And there were two disciples named Judas. One of these was known as Judas Iscariot. He was put in charge of the purse they shared. If Judas ever went missing, everyone knew it would be something to do with money. Why not? He was good at that sort of thing, and everyone trusted him to be honest...

ALL ABOUT LOVE

O ne day, a huge crowd gathered on a hillside to listen to Jesus.

"Is there anyone here who knows they need God's help and forgiveness?" he asked. "They can count on God's blessing.

"My message is about helping people live as God's friends.

"Don't give in to anger. Don't think about getting revenge. Instead, show love and kindness to everyone – even those who have been unkind to you.

"And don't spend your life fretting about money and all the things it can buy. Instead, make it your aim to live as God wants, as members of God's kingdom.

"Look at the birds: they don't sow seed or harvest crops, yet God provides food for them.

"Look at the flowers: they don't spin thread nor stitch cloth, yet God clothes them in petals lovelier than clothes.

"If God takes such care of the birds and flowers, you can be sure that God will take care of you."

ALL ABOUT FORGIVENESS

Forgiveness was at the heart of Jesus' teaching.

"Remember to do for others exactly what you would want them to do for you," he told his listeners.

"Do good to others without expecting anything back, remembering that God showers blessings on bad people as well as good people.

"Do not judge others, and God will not judge you.

"Do not condemn others, and God will not condemn you.

"Forgive others, and God will forgive you.

"Perhaps you think someone doesn't see things the way they should: it's as if they have a speck of something in their eye.

"Don't criticize them for it or try to put them right.

"Instead, think about the way you see things. They may have a speck in their eye – but you might have a log in yours!

"Put yourself right before you start trying to change others!"

THE TWO BUILDERS

Jesus' listeners were an enthusiastic crowd. After all, they'd made the effort to come and listen to him... and the things he said were interesting.

But would it change the way they lived their lives?

Jesus gave them a clear warning: "It's not enough to claim to be a follower of mine," he said. "It's not enough to come and listen. You have to obey my teaching.

"If you do, you are like the man who built his house on rock. He worked hard, he dug deep foundations. When the rain came and the river flooded, his house was safe.

"If you don't obey my teaching, you are like the man who built his house on sand. When the rain came, and the river flooded, his house fell down flat.

"What a crash!"

THE PARABLE OF THE SOWER

A large crowd gathered on the shore of Lake Galilee. Jesus took his place in a moored boat and began to preach.

"Once," he said, "a man went to scatter seed in his field.

"Some fell on the path. At once birds came and pecked it up.

"Some fell on rocky ground. The seedlings grew but their roots could not go deep. When the sun grew hot, the plants wilted.

"Some seed fell among thorn bushes. The stronger plants choked the seedlings' growth.

"Some fell on good soil and produced a harvest: some thirty grains, some sixty, and some a hundred."

THE MEANING OF THE PARABLE

Jesus' story left even his disciples puzzled.

"It is about God's kingdom," Jesus explained.

"The seed on the path is like people who barely hear my words. At once the Evil One snatches them away.

"The seed on rocky ground is like those who become enthusiastic about my teaching. Then obeying it gets tough and they give up.

"The seed among thorns is like those who dream of being my followers but who let everyday things get in the way.

"The seed on good soil is like those who hear my teaching, who obey it, and whose lives bear fruit."

JESUS AND

Jesus spent all day preaching to the crowds from his boat. As the sun set, he called his disciples.

"Let's travel on," he said. "Tomorrow we can be on the other side of the lake."

As they set sail, Jesus fell asleep in the bottom of the boat.

The night grew dark. The clouds billowed in the night-time sky.

Then the wind began to blow and the waves began to crash.

THE STORM AT SEA

"Wake up!" the disciples called to Jesus. "Don't you care? We're all about to drown."

Jesus stood up. "Be quiet," he said to the wind. "Be still," he said to the waves.

At once the sea was calm.

"Why were you afraid?" asked Jesus. "Have you no faith?"

That scared the disciples. "Who can he BE that he can do such things?" they whispered.

JAIRUS AND HIS DAUGHTER

As Jesus and his friends sailed into one of the lakeside towns, crowds of people jostled on the quayside.

A man named Jairus came and threw himself at Jesus' feet.

"Please help me," he begged. "My daughter is dying."

Jesus agreed to come, but it was slow going. The crowds elbowed and pushed. A woman touched Jesus in the hope of being made well, and Jesus both healed her and stopped to talk.

Then a messenger arrived. "I'm sorry," he whispered to Jairus. "You don't need to bother the preacher now. Your daughter – she has just died."

Jesus overheard. "Don't be afraid," he said. "Believe in me."

He walked to Jairus's house. He sent away the women who had come to weep and wail.

He went to the room where the child's frail body lay.

Taking a slender, pale hand, he simply said, "Little girl, get up."

To the astonishment of both Jairus and his wife, the girl sat up.

"Now it is for you to take good care of her," said Jesus.

FEEDING THE

One day, Jesus and his disciples went off to spend a day away from the crowds.

Then someone spotted where they were going, and the news spread.

When they reached the chosen spot, Jesus found himself facing an eager crowd. He welcomed them all, and spent the day preaching and healing.

Then the sun began to go down.

"It's time to send the people away," the disciples said to Jesus. "They'll need to find food and a place to stay."

"You should give them something," replied Jesus.

"Surely we can't," replied Andrew. "There's a young lad here who has five loaves and two fish, but that won't feed this many people."

FIVE THOUSAND

"Tell the people to sit down," replied Jesus.
As the crowd settled, Jesus took the loaves
and fish and said a prayer of thanksgiving. 
Then he began to share it out.
Each person had all they wanted.
When the meal was over, the disciples filled twelve baskets
with the scraps.

WHO IS THE GREATEST?

One day, Jesus' disciples had a big argument.
This one and that one claimed to be the most important disciple, the one the others should look up to.

Jesus found out, and he was not impressed.

He brought a child from among the crowd and stood him by his side.

"Anyone who welcomes this child in my name welcomes me," he said. "And if you welcome me, you are welcoming the One who sent me.

"Remember this: the one who is least among you all is the greatest."

The disciples heard his words, but did they really listen?

JESUS AND THE CHILDREN

Sometime later, a group of mothers came to Jesus bringing their little children.

"We'd like the preacher to say a blessing prayer for them," they said.

"Our master is far too busy for that," scolded the disciples.

But Jesus overheard them.

"Let the children come to me, and do not try to stop them," he said. "The kingdom of God belongs to such as these."

WHO IS MY NEIGHBOUR?

A teacher of the Law once came to Jesus with a question. He was hoping it would catch Jesus out.

"Teacher," he said smarmily, "what must I do to have eternal life?"

Jesus replied with a question: "What do our Scriptures say?"

"Ah," said the teacher, happy to show off his knowledge. "It can be summed up like this: 'Love the Lord your God with all your heart, with all your soul, with all your strength, and with all your mind', and 'Love your neighbour as you love yourself'."

"Quite right," said Jesus. "Obey those commands and you will have the eternal life you seek."

The teacher was annoyed not to have made Jesus explain his own teaching. "Who is my neighbour?" he asked.

Jesus replied with a story:

"There was once a man who was going from Jerusalem to Jericho.

"As he walked the lonely road through open country, bandits leaped. They beat him, took all he had, and left him for dead.

"Who would be a good neighbour and help him?"

175

THE GOOD SAMARITAN

J *esus continued his story:*

"The next person to come along the road was a priest from the Temple. He saw the body and was horrified.
"But he didn't want to touch it, so he walked by on the other side of the road.

"Next came one of the helpers in the Temple. He walked up to the body and shuddered. Fearfully he hurried on.

"Then a Samaritan came by."

The teacher of the Law grimaced. Samaritans were outsiders. They didn't understand God's laws at all!

"The Samaritan stopped," said Jesus. "He bandaged the injured man's wounds and lifted him onto his own donkey.

"He led him to an inn to rest the night. In the morning, he paid the innkeeper to go on looking after him until he was well.

"Now," said Jesus, "which of the passers-by was neighbour to the man?"

"The one who was kind to him," replied the teacher.

Jesus replied, "You go, then, and do the same."

THE TWO SISTERS

One day, Jesus and his disciples came to a village where they had friends. Two sisters, Mary and Martha, welcomed them into their home.

Mary was eager to learn about Jesus' teaching. As soon as he sat down and began to preach, she was at his feet and listening to his every word.

Martha was busy with household chores. There is so much to do when there are guests: making sure everyone has somewhere to sit, bringing drinks, preparing a meal.

And still Mary just sat; and listened.

In the end Martha could stand it no more. She marched over to Jesus. "Don't you care that my sister has left me to do all the work by myself? I want you to tell her to come and help me!"

"Poor Martha!" replied Jesus, kindly. "You are worried about so many things, but only one thing is important. Mary has made the right choice in choosing to listen to me."

HOW TO PRAY

*J*esus often spent time alone praying to God. One day,
when he returned to his disciples, they made a request:
"Please teach us to pray."
Jesus gave them this prayer:

Our Father in heaven,
hallowed be your name,
your kingdom come,
your will be done,
on earth as in heaven.
Give us today our daily bread.
Forgive us our sins
as we forgive those who sin against us.
Lead us not into temptation
but deliver us from evil.

"Imagine you need something from a neighbour," continued Jesus. "Say you need to borrow some bread to feed a friend who has arrived late at night. You'll keep knocking at the door until you get what you need.

"So if that works – imagine how much more God wants to give you the things you need.

"Ask, and you will receive.

"Seek, and you will find.

"Knock, and the door will be opened."

THE RICH FOOL

I s money the most important thing in the world? Jesus didn't think so, and told this story:

"There was once a man whose land produced wonderful crops. As one good harvest followed another, he began to worry.

"'I'm running out of space to store my grain. Whatever shall I do?

"'Ah! Of course! I'll tear down my old barns and build bigger ones.

"'That way I'll be able to store all my crops and all my riches.

"'Then I'll be able to retire from work. I'll be able to eat, drink, and enjoy myself.'

"That night, in a dream, God warned him. 'You fool. Tonight is the night you die. Now someone else will inherit all you have.'"

Jesus looked at his listeners. "Don't make that mistake," he said. "Don't set your heart on getting rich, but rather on living as God's friends, in God's kingdom.

"That way, you will store up riches in heaven that will last for eternity."

THE TEN BRIDESMAIDS

"If you want to be part of God's kingdom," Jesus told his listeners, "you must live as God wants all the time.

"There were once ten bridesmaids. They all waited outside the bride's house with lit oil lamps, ready to light the bridegroom's way.

"They had all filled their lamps with enough oil to last several hours.

"The sun set and the evening wore on. All the women began to nod off. The lamps flickered and burned low.

"Around midnight, there came a shout. 'The bridegroom is coming.'

"All the women jumped up.

"Five of them were ready with extra oil. They refilled their lamps so the flames burned brightly.

"The other five had no more oil, and their lamps were about to flicker out.

"They hurried to fetch more... but too late. When they came back, they found themselves locked out of the feast.

"So always be ready for God's kingdom to come," Jesus said. "You don't know when it will happen."

THE MUSTARD SEED

J esus' disciples wanted to understand better what he
meant by the kingdom of God.

"Let me try to explain," said Jesus.

"It is like a man who takes a mustard seed – a tiny, tiny
seed – and plants it in the ground.

"All unseen, it begins to grow.

"Time passes, and it becomes a mighty tree.
All the birds of the air come and nest in its branches."

THE GREAT FEAST

One day, a Pharisee invited Jesus for a meal. The man himself was highly respected, and many of his guests thought they were important people too.

Jesus told a story:

"There was once a man who was planning a great feast. Everyone he asked was delighted to get an invitation.

"On the day of the feast, the man sent his servant to summon the guests.

"One by one they began to make excuses.

"'Oh dear, I've just bought a field, and must go and look at it.'

"'I've bought five new pairs of oxen. I simply must try them out.'

"'I've just got married. I'm really too busy now.'

"The servant went and told his master.

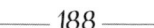

"'That's enraging!' cried the man. 'Listen: go into town, and fetch the poor, the blind, and those who cannot walk.'

"The servant went, and many people came.

"'There is still room for many more,' said the man. 'Now go out into the country lanes and tell anyone you find to come.

"'I want my house to be full... but those who turned me down won't get a look in.'"

THE LOST SHEEP

One day, a crowd of tax collectors and other less-than-respectable people came to listen to Jesus.

The Pharisees and the rabbis started grumbling to each other.

"What kind of teacher can he be if he welcomes this rabble?"

Jesus told a story.

"There was once a shepherd who had a hundred sheep.

"So he was surprised when he counted them to find only ninety-nine. What should he do?

"At once he left the ninety-nine safely grazing in the pasture and set off to find his lost sheep. He didn't mind the rough path, nor the thorny bushes, nor the wearying heat. He kept on looking until he found his lost sheep.

"Carefully he picked it up and carried it home.

"When it was safe with the flock again, he called his friends around for a celebration.

"You can be sure of this: when one person who has lost their way is brought back onto the right path, all heaven sings for joy."

THE LOST SON

"Once," said Jesus, "there was a man who had two sons. Together they worked the family farm.

"Then the younger son wanted to live life his own way. He went to his father.

"'One day I'll inherit my share of what you own,' he said. 'I'll be old then. I want it now.'

"With a heavy heart, the father agreed. The young man took the money and went off to a country far away and spent it all just partying.

"Then famine struck. The price of food shot up.

"The young man needed a job. But he was just a farmer's boy, and he was lucky to get work looking after a herd of pigs.

"He got paid almost nothing. He could hardly afford food. He was so hungry that the pig's food looked tempting.

"'I've made a huge mistake,' he said to himself.

"'I shall give up this job and go back to my father. I can't expect him to treat me as a son, but perhaps he'll take me on as a servant.'

THE HOMECOMING

"*Every day, in the evening, the father went up to the flat roof of the farmhouse. He sat in the shade of a fig tree and wondered about his younger son.*

"*Then, one evening, he saw... it couldn't be... but maybe... yes, surely, it was his son!*

"*The father rushed to greet him and threw his arms around him.*

"*Through the hug, the young man began his speech: 'Father,* he said, *'what I did was wrong. I don't deserve to be called your son anymore.'*

"*The father wasn't listening.*

"'Less of that,' he said. 'What matters is that you're back.'

"He began calling to the servants. 'Hurry, we're going to have a party. I want the best food... and a clean outfit for this young man! Quick, jump to it!'

"The older son was furious to see how his good-for-nothing brother had been welcomed.

"'Don't be angry!' urged the father. 'Everything I have is yours.

"'But tonight we must be happy – the one who was lost has been found.'"

THE PHARISEE AND

Some of the people who came to listen to Jesus were very religious. They could also be very smug. Jesus told them this story.

"Once, two men went to the Temple to pray: a Pharisee and a tax collector.

"The Pharisee stood apart from everyone else and said this:

"'Thank you, God, that I am not like other people. I am not greedy or dishonest, I am faithful in my marriage, I keep all your laws...

"'My life is so different from that of the tax collector over there.'

THE TAX COLLECTOR

"The tax collector stayed at the back of the crowd. He thought of all the things he had done that made him feel ashamed.

"'God, have mercy on me, a sinner,' he said.

"You can be sure of this," Jesus said. "It was the tax collector who mended his friendship with God by his prayer.

"So don't think too highly of yourselves. God welcomes those who are humble."

THE MAN IN THE TREE

Zacchaeus was just about the least popular man in Jericho.

And why? Because he was a tax collector who had made his money by overcharging honest taxpayers.

So when the crowds gathered to welcome Jesus, no one let Zacchaeus through to the front. It was no use him pleading that he was too short to see. No one cared.

Zacchaeus shinned up a tree. Hidden among the leaves, he could see and not be seen.

But then Jesus stopped under the tree and looked right up at him.

"Come down," he called to Zacchaeus. "I want to come to your house."

Zacchaeus scrambled down and welcomed his guest with the best of everything.

Whatever Jesus said to the man had a big impact. After the meal, the cheating tax collector stood up and made an announcement.

"I'm going to give half of what I have to the poor, and I'm going to repay anyone I've cheated four times as much."

Jesus smiled: "My job is to find people who have made wrong choices and set them on the right path," he said.

RIDING TO JERUSALEM

The time came for the Passover festival. Jesus decided to go with his disciples to Jerusalem.

As he came near the city, he borrowed a donkey so he could ride.

The crowds saw him and began to whisper. "Look – it's Jesus! And he's riding, not walking like he usually does."

"Maybe he's going to declare himself to be our people's new leader."

"He's already got a huge following."

People began to cheer and shout. "God bless the king! God bless the chosen king."

Some cut palm branches and waved them like flags.

Others threw their cloaks on the ground to make a carpet for the donkey to walk on.

A group of Pharisees heard the uproar. They were outraged and marched up to Jesus.

"Tell your mob to be quiet!" they demanded.

"I tell you this," replied Jesus. "If I could make them be silent, the stones themselves would start shouting."

THE TEMPLE COURTYARD

When Jesus reached Jerusalem, he went to the Temple. The courtyard was full of noise and bustle: people had set up market stalls for the festival. They were selling animals to be bought as offerings, and changing money into Temple coins.

Jesus frowned. Then he began to drive the stallholders out.

"This is meant to be a place of prayer," he cried. "You have turned it into a den of thieves."

THE WIDOW'S GIFT

In the days that followed, Jesus went to the Temple to preach.

"Beware of the rabbis," he said. "They expect people to think highly of them and their long prayers, but they insist on the letter of the Law even if it robs poor widows of their homes."

He looked around and saw rich people coming to the collecting boxes to make their gifts of money.

Then a poor widow came and quietly she dropped in two small coins.

"Look at that!" exclaimed Jesus. "The rich people could afford to make their offering, but hers has cost her all she had."

JUDAS ISCARIOT

Jesus' arrival had caused a real stir in Jerusalem.

It was not all good: the rabbis and the Temple priests whispered that Jesus was a dangerous nuisance.

"How can we get rid of him?" they wondered. "The crowds adore him."

Then came the chance they were looking for. One of Jesus' own disciples, Judas Iscariot, met them in secret. He offered to tell them when and how they could find Jesus when he was alone.

In return for the information, Judas accepted thirty pieces of silver.

A NEW COMMANDMENT

At the heart of the Passover festival was a shared meal. As Jesus gathered with his disciples in an upstairs room, he did something surprising.

He put on an apron and began to wash his disciples' dusty feet, as a servant might.

"I am your Teacher," he explained, "but I have served you humbly.

"I want you to treat one another in the same way.

"And now I am giving you a new commandment: love one another."

THE LAST SUPPER

Jesus and his disciples took their place at the supper table. "I have been looking forward to sharing the Passover meal with you all," said Jesus. "There are hard times ahead for me, but when those are over, this celebration will have a new meaning in God's kingdom."

He took a piece of bread and said a thanksgiving prayer. Then he broke the bread and shared it.

"This is my body, which is for you," he said. "Do this in memory of me."

After supper he took the cup of wine.

"This cup is God's new covenant, sealed with my blood," he said. "Whenever you drink it, do so in memory of me."

He looked around at his friends and sighed. "I already know that one of you is going to betray me."

Peter shook his head. "It won't be me!" he said. "You can always count on me."

Jesus looked at him sternly. "Before the night is over, you will have denied knowing me three times," he warned.

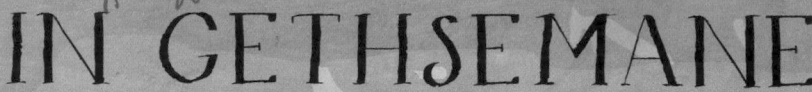

IN GETHSEMANE

When the Passover supper was over, Jesus and his disciples went to an olive grove: the garden of Gethsemane.

"We're all going to be put to the test tonight," said Jesus. "You had better start praying that you won't fail."

He went off by himself. "Father God, please don't make me suffer," he prayed, "though of course, I will do whatever you require."

He went back to his disciples. In spite of his warning, they had all fallen asleep.

"Get up!" he whispered. "What did I tell you?"

Even as he was speaking, armed men appeared out of the shadows.

Among them was Judas Iscariot. He walked up to Jesus, as if to greet him with a kiss.

Jesus shook his head. "So this is how you betray me," he said sadly. Then he turned to his loyal disciples.

"Don't fight," he said.

He didn't struggle as the armed men grabbed him. "You didn't dare do this in the open, did you?" he chided. "Truly, this is the hour when darkness rules."

IN THE HOUSE OF

Armed men marched Jesus off to the high priest's house. Peter followed, dodging among the shadows so as not to be seen.

He sidled into the courtyard and joined the servants who were sitting around a fire.

One of the women watched as he sat down. She pointed her finger.

THE HIGH PRIEST

"Look at him!" she exclaimed. "He was one of Jesus' followers!"

"Pah!" retorted Peter. "I don't even know the man."

A little while later, another servant came by. He stopped in surprise. "Hey, you!" he called to Peter. "You were one of Jesus' crowd!"

"No, I wasn't!" growled Peter.

For an hour or so he ignored the whispering around him. Then another man came and accused him directly. "You must be one of Jesus' friends. Your Galilean accent gives you away."

"I don't know what you're talking about." Peter shouted his reply and stormed off.

A cockerel crowed the dawn. Peter realized he had indeed denied knowing Jesus three times before the night was over. He put his head in his hands and wept.

JESUS ON TRIAL

T he morning after Jesus' arrest, he was put on trial in the
high priest's house. The chief priests and rabbis had one
big question:

"Are you the messiah, the Christ, God's chosen king?"

"You won't believe me, whatever I say," replied Jesus.

It was true: the council members had already decided Jesus
was guilty.

They marched their prisoner to the Roman governor,
Pontius Pilate, and asked him to pass the death sentence.

"This man claims to be our people's king," they said. "He is

telling people not to obey Roman laws."

Pilate was not convinced. He looked at the crowds who had gathered outside. They had come to make the traditional Passover request for a prisoner to be set free. Surely they would rescue the popular preacher?

"Shall I set Jesus free?" he asked them.

To his dismay, he found a hostile mob. They asked for another prisoner to be freed – a known murderer, in fact.

"What about Jesus?" asked Pilate.

"Crucify him!" they cried.

JESUS IS CRUCIFIED

Pilate wrote out the notice of Jesus' supposed crime so it could be nailed to the cross above him:

"Jesus of Nazareth, the king of the Jews"

He ordered his soldiers to carry out the execution.

They in turn loaded a cross on to Jesus' shoulders. They marched him out of Jerusalem, along with two other prisoners. On a hill named Golgotha, they crucified all three men.

While the soldiers gambled among themselves for who should claim Jesus' clothes, Jesus' own mother walked up to the cross. By her side was the faithful disciple named John.

"Take care of my mother," said Jesus to the young man.
To his mother he said, "John will be your son now."
Then he gasped. "I'm thirsty!"
Someone dipped a sponge in wine and passed it up to
him on a stick. Jesus was able to drink just a few drops.
"It is finished," he said, and died.

BURIED IN A TOMB

Among Jesus' followers was a man named Joseph, who came from the town of Arimathea. He had kept his faith in the young preacher a secret: respectable men like him did not want to fall out with the authorities.

However, because Jesus had died an unjust death, Joseph stepped forward. He went to Pilate and asked for permission to take the body.

Then he and a friend named Nicodemus took the body down. They covered it in the traditional spices, wrapped it in linen, and took it to a rock-cut tomb in a garden.

Such was their sorrow they hardly noticed more of Jesus' followers watching as they placed the body inside the tomb and rolled the stone door shut.

The sun was setting. The sabbath day of rest was about to begin. Sadly and silently, Jesus' friends went their separate ways.

THE EMPTY TOMB

O n the Sunday morning, while it was still dark, Mary
Magdalene went to the tomb.

To her dismay, she saw that the door had been rolled open.

She hurried off to tell the disciples, and returned with Peter
and John. Both men peered inside. The tomb was empty,
except for the cloths that had been wrapped around the body.

Puzzled, they went away, leaving Mary alone and weeping.
As she looked into the tomb, she saw angels, dressed in white.
"Why are you crying?" they asked her.

"Because they've taken the body of my Lord Jesus," she said. "I don't know where it is."

She turned around and saw a man. "That must be the gardener," she thought. "I'll ask him about the body."

As she did, the man turned. "Mary," he said.

It was then that she recognized him. "Jesus!" she cried. He was alive!

THE LOCKED ROOM

It was late on the Sunday evening. The eleven faithful disciples had gone into hiding together. When Thomas went out on an errand, they locked the door behind him.

Suddenly, Jesus came and stood among them.

He gave the everyday greeting: "Peace be with you."

Then he showed them the wounds of his crucifixion – in his hands and in his side.

"Peace be with you," he said again. "As my Father God sent me, so now I send you to all the world with my message."

THOMAS

When Thomas returned to the disciples, he was dismayed at what they told him.

"I don't believe you," he told them firmly, "and unless I see Jesus with my own eyes and touch his scarred hands and side, I won't."

A week went by. Again the disciples were together in a locked room. Jesus came and spoke directly to Thomas.

"Look," he said, "here are my hands. Reach out and touch them – and the wound in my side as well."

Thomas's reply was simple: "My Lord and my God," he said.

IN GALILEE

Jesus' disciples were afraid. The same people who had had Jesus crucified must surely be looking for them.

Peter and six others decided to leave Jerusalem for Galilee.

There, Peter made an announcement. "I'm going fishing," he said.

"We'll come with you," agreed the others.

They fished all night, but they caught nothing.

As they sailed back to shore, a man stood waving at them. "Throw the net out on the right," he called.

They did so – and at once the net was full of fish.

John said to Peter, "It's Jesus!" – and Peter jumped out of the boat to swim to shore.

Jesus had some fish cooking over a fire, and bread to share. After they had eaten, Jesus spoke quietly to Peter.

"Do you love me?" he asked.

"You know I do," replied Peter.

Jesus asked again – and again: as many times as Peter had denied Jesus on the dark night of his arrest.

"You know I love you," Peter insisted.

"Then take care of my followers, my flock of sheep," he said.

INTO HEAVEN

Jesus met with his faithful disciples one last time.

"This is what I want you to do," he told them. "Go to all people everywhere and invite them to be my followers too.

"Baptize them in the name of God the Father, God the Son, and God the Holy Spirit.

"Teach them to obey everything I have told you.

"For this you will need the help and strength of God's Holy Spirit. Stay in Jerusalem until that happens."

As Jesus finished speaking, he vanished into the clouds. The disciples peered upwards, not understanding.

Then two men dressed in white appeared at their side.

"Why are you looking at the sky?" they asked. "Jesus has been taken into heaven. One day he will return in the same way you saw him go."

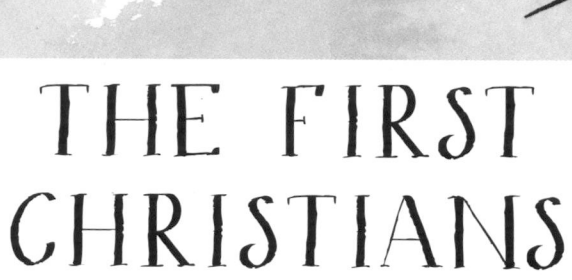

THE FIRST CHRISTIANS

When Jesus went back to heaven, his disciples felt more uncertain than ever.

What chance did they have to spread the news about God's kingdom?

Then they learned to trust in God. They preached boldly, and many listened and believed what they said. They believed that Jesus was the saviour God had promised: the messiah, the Christ. Soon they became known as Christians.

The new Christians in turn began to spread the message – and not just to Jews. They went and preached to people all over the Roman empire. There were good roads for overland travel. There were shipping routes that made it possible to go to islands and faraway shores.

One of Jesus' followers wrote these words to encourage Christians in their faith:

Dear friends. Let us love one another, because love comes from God....

This is what love is: it is not that we have loved God, but that he loved us.

1 JOHN 4

THE DAY OF PENTECOST

I t was the harvest festival called Pentecost. Pilgrims from countries far and wide had come to Jerusalem to celebrate.

Jesus' followers were still living in fear. They had gathered in a room together to encourage one another.

Suddenly they heard a noise like a rushing wind, and they saw what looked like flames dancing above their heads. God's Holy Spirit filled them with joy and gave them the ability to talk in all kinds of different languages.

Delighted and astonished, they tumbled out into the street.

PETER'S SERMON

The crowds laughed.

"Are these people drunk?" they asked. "Is that how they're speaking in so many different languages?"

Peter stood up and spoke boldly. "We're not drunk," he explained. "It's only nine o'clock in the morning!

"We have been given power from God to tell you all about Jesus. He was crucified here in Jerusalem, but God has raised him to life. He is the promised messiah, the Christ, and you need to pay attention to his message."

As a result of Peter's preaching, three thousand people asked to be baptized as followers of Jesus.

A MIRACLE
BY THE TEMPLE

One day, Peter and John went to the Temple for prayer. There was a man waiting outside the entrance gate who could not walk.

"Could you spare some money?" he begged.

"I haven't got any money," replied Peter, "but I can offer you something else. In the name of Jesus Christ, get up and walk."

He took the man by the hand and helped him to his feet.

Astonished, the man took a step... and another.

"I can walk!" he cried. "I'm healed... oh, hallelujah!"

A crowd quickly gathered.

"See what has happened," Peter told them. "It is the power of God that has cured this man – the same God who sent his Son, Jesus, to help us. So believe in Jesus and his message: that everyone should turn away from wrongdoing and enjoy God's blessing."

The Temple priests arrested Peter and John and told them not to preach any more dangerous nonsense. But the disciples would not be silenced... and the number of new believers just kept on growing.

STEPHEN THE MARTYR

As the number of believers grew, the disciples chose people who were both wise and kind to help take care of them; among them was a young man named Stephen.

Stephen was able to speak very clearly about his new faith, and what he said made some people angry.

They dragged him before the Council of religious leaders to make their complaint that he had said things about the Jewish faith that were disrespectful.

Stephen was invited to reply.

"Time and again our people have failed to recognize God's messengers," he said. "Now you are the stubborn ones, who simply can't see that Jesus is the greatest of God's messengers."

His words made the Council furious. They rushed at him and dragged him outside the walls of Jerusalem.

There they flung off their cloaks and left them in a heap under the watchful eye of a young scholar named Saul.

Saul watched, smiling grimly, as the men hurled stones at Stephen. He was pleased to see him dead.

SAUL SEES THE LIGHT

*S*aul was troubled. So many people were becoming
followers of Jesus! He was a scholar of the Jewish
scriptures, and the new teaching seemed all wrong.

He went to the high priest in Jerusalem.

"I'd like your permission to go to Damascus," he said.
"I'll find all the Christians there and have them arrested."

The high priest agreed, and Saul set out on the long journey
north.

As he and his companions were getting near Damascus,
Saul saw a flash of light. He heard a voice:

"Saul, why do you treat me so cruelly?" it said.

"Who are you?" cried Saul.

"I am Jesus," came the reply. "Now get up, and go to the
city. There you will be told what to do."

Saul blinked. The light had gone… but now he could
not see. "Help me," he begged his companions. "Take me to
Damascus. Find a safe place for me to stay."

His campaign against the believers was not going to plan.

A CHANGE OF HEART

Ananias was one of the Christians in Damascus. One day, he heard God speaking to him.

"Ananias, go to Straight Street and find a man named Saul, from the city of Tarsus. Place your hands on him and pray that he will be able to see again."

"Dear God!" replied Ananias in astonishment. "I dare not do that. Saul is here to arrest believers like me."

"I have chosen Saul to spread the news about Jesus beyond the Jewish community, to the Gentiles," replied God.

So Ananias went. He healed Saul and began teaching him all about Jesus.

Saul had a complete change of heart. He in turn began to preach about Jesus.

Other Jews in the city were confused and angry. "He came to arrest the Christians," they complained. "The time has come for us to arrest him!"

Other Christians heard of their plan. One night, they helped Saul escape over the city walls... hiding in a basket lowered on ropes.

It was to be the first of many adventures!

PETER AND THE SOLDIER

Peter was doing just as Jesus had asked: he was going from place to place spreading the new Christian faith.

One day, when he was staying in Joppa, he went on to the flat roof to pray.

As he prayed, he fell into a kind of dream. He saw a something like a large sheet coming from the heavens. In it were all kinds of animals.

A voice spoke: "Here is food for you to kill and eat," it said.

"I can't do that!" said Peter. "All these animals are ones that we Jews are forbidden to eat. We call them 'unclean'."

"If God tells you something is clean you mustn't call it unclean," came the reply.

Peter was puzzling about what the dream meant when messengers arrived to see him.

A Roman centurion in nearby

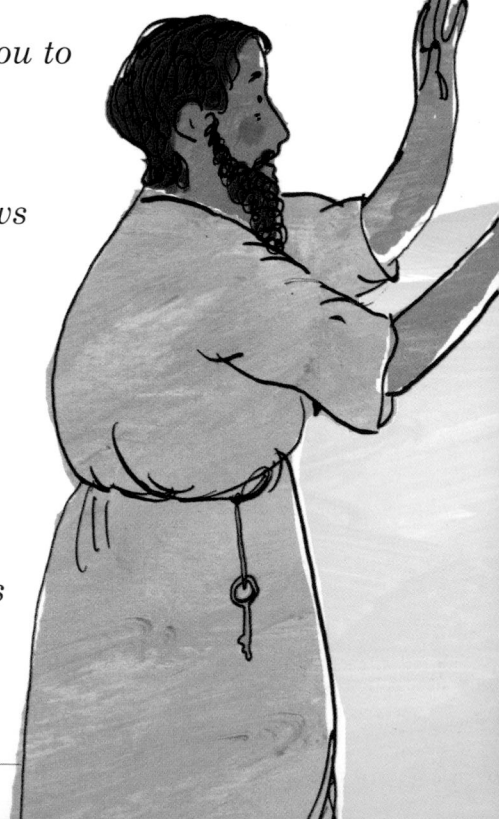

Caesarea wanted Peter to come and preach to him.

Peter agreed to go. As he made his way to the house of Captain Cornelius, he understood: the dream was God's way of telling him to break out of the old Jewish traditions. The message about Jesus was for everyone!

PAUL THE APOSTLE

*T*he new groups of Christians faced quite a challenge. Many Jews disliked them, fearing they were disrespectful of their faith and traditions.

Many non-Jews eyed them warily, wondering if they were showing proper respect for Roman laws and traditions.

But these problems didn't stop the Christians. Those who lived in the city of Antioch even set up a special fund to send preachers to faraway places. Saul was now such a keen Christian he was chosen to be the missionary. Wherever he went, he introduced himself by the Roman version of his name: Paul.

Wherever he and his companions went, they convinced many people to put their trust in Jesus. Those who were wealthy offered their homes as a place where the believers could meet: masters and slaves, Jews and Gentiles, all together.

241

PAUL IN PRISON

One day, Paul was in the city of Philippi with his companions. He came across a young slave who wasn't in her right mind and healed her of her madness.

The woman's owners were furious. "Her rantings were valuable," they cried. "We sold her services as a fortune teller!"

They dragged Paul and his friend Silas to the city authorities in the public square.

"These Jewish preachers are just troublemakers!" they said. "We want them punished."

Paul and Silas were whipped and thrown into jail.

The two men were sitting in their cell singing hymns through the night... when an earthquake struck.

"Don't worry!" Paul cried to the jailer. "Neither I nor anyone else is going to try to escape. You won't be in trouble... and I'll tell you about the most important thing of all: believing in Jesus."

Because of Paul's preaching, even the jailer became a Christian.

As for the rest of the punishment, the city authorities let Paul and Silas go. They even said sorry for having thrown them in prison.

THE RIOT IN EPHESUS

O ne of the places where Paul preached was the city of Ephesus. This greatly angered a silversmith named Demetrius, who called his fellow silversmiths to a meeting.

"We all know that Ephesus is famous for its shrine to the goddess Diana," he began. "That's why so many tourists come. And what do they all buy? The gorgeous little silver models of the goddess that we make.

"The last thing we want is people switching faith and becoming Christians. The preaching of that awful Paul is an insult to our beloved goddess."

His words got the silversmiths all fired up. "Great is Diana of the Ephesians!" they cried. The crowd around them took up their words.

"Diana! Diana!" they echoed.

"Get those Christians over there," shouted others.

The mob seized two of Paul's companions and dragged them to the huge open-air theatre. If the town clerk had not come and demanded calm, who knows what would have happened to them!

"These Christians have not done anything wrong," declared the clerk. "You must let them go."

PAUL

Paul was determined to travel far and wide preaching about Jesus. At the same time, he wanted to take good care of the groups of believers that had formed in all the different towns and cities.

So he wrote them letters: words of wisdom and encouragement that could be read aloud.

Here is part of what he wrote to the new believers in Corinth:

"It doesn't matter how well I speak, unless I show love in all I do.

"Words are just noise – like a clanging gong or a noisy cymbal.

"I may be learned, I may have great faith, I may face trials and persecution boldly – but none of this matters unless I show love in all I do.

"Love is patient and kind; it is not jealous or conceited or proud; love is not ill-mannered or selfish

THE LETTER WRITER

or irritable; love does not keep a record of wrongs; love is not happy with evil, but is happy with the truth. Love never gives up; and its faith, hope, and patience never fail.

"The things that seem important now will all fade in the light of eternity... except for three: faith, hope, and love; and the greatest of these is love."

PAUL on TRIAL

A ll over the Roman empire, the number of people who
believed in Jesus was growing. Paul's tireless work as a
preacher was bearing fruit.

But it was also making him many enemies. One day, Paul
asked his companions to make the next bit of their journey
– from Troas to Miletus – by boat. He himself walked alone
along the coastal path before joining them. It gave him time
to think of the troubles that lay ahead.

He knew it was right to go back to Jerusalem, to meet with
the elders of the church there. That way he could help Jewish
Christians and Gentile Christians to understand one another.

But Paul would not be safe there. Enemies would lie in wait: to find fault, to have him arrested, to have him put on trial.

Paul gazed out on the glittering turquoise sea. Once, in the shadows of Gethsemane, Jesus had had to make a choice – to face his enemies or to run away. Jesus had not run away; nor would Paul.

SHIPWRECK

Paul was right to be anxious. When he reached Jerusalem, the Jewish authorities were waiting for their chance to arrest him.

Paul spoke to the army commander in charge in Jerusalem. "I know my fellow Jews want to put me on trial," he said, "but they won't treat me fairly.

"I am a Roman citizen. I want to plead my case in the emperor's court, in Rome."

After many delays, Paul was put on a boat bound for Rome, along with other prisoners.

It was late in the year. Stormy weather battered the ship for days on end, but the captain was determined to keep going.

"And I believe God wants me to preach in Rome," declared Paul confidently. "I'm sure we'll get there!"

One morning, the sailors saw a misty coastline. Desperately they tried to drive the ship toward a beach. They hit a sandbank. The boat began to break up.

Paul and everyone on board had to swim for their lives. Everyone made it safely to shore: not Rome, but the island of Malta. There they were made welcome through the stormy winter.

PAUL IN ROME

In the spring, a boat arrived to rescue those who had been shipwrecked. At long last Paul reached Rome.

The Christians there welcomed the famous preacher. Paul lived under house arrest until a date for his trial could be set.

One useful way to spend the time was writing letters to the churches he had helped set up. He also wrote letters to friends he had made along the way – including one named Philemon, in the city of Colossae.

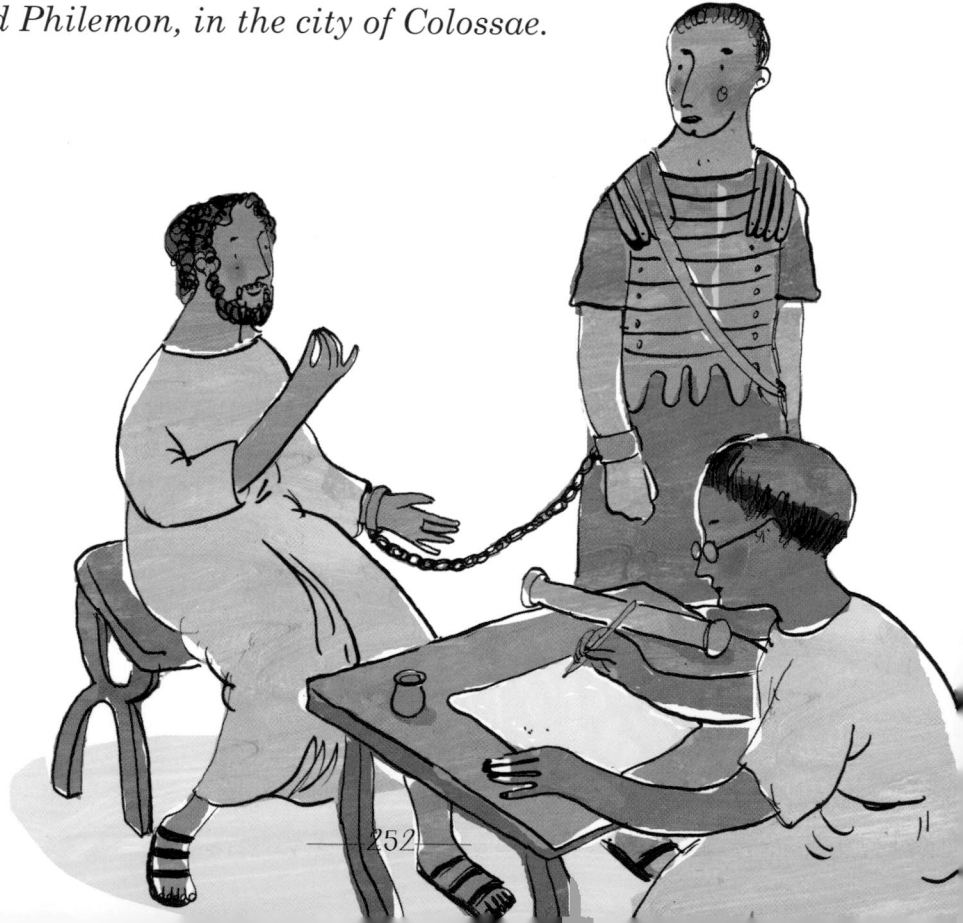

Dear Philemon,

I always remember you in my prayers. I hear lots of good things about the group of Christians that meets in your house.

I'm sending this letter by special messenger: your runaway slave Onesimus. He's become a Christian now, and he's been a great help to me here in Rome. Please welcome him back into your household – not just as a slave, but as a brother in Christ.

Oh – and if he owes you any money, please let me pay the debt.

Greetings to everyone, and I hope to come and see you soon.

May the grace of the Lord Jesus Christ be with you all.

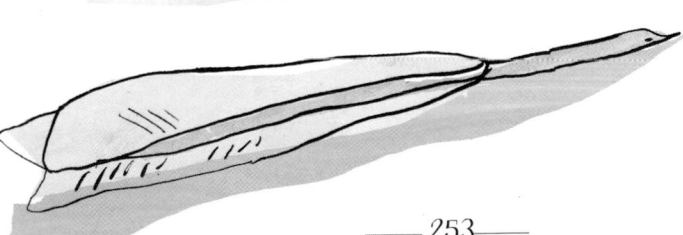

A NEW BEGINNING

Every time Paul met with the Christians in Rome, and heard news from far and wide, he could be sure of one thing:

All over the empire, people were becoming Christians, and learning to follow Jesus.

Troubles lay ahead: in the years to come, Christians would be persecuted for their faith and would die cruel and horrible deaths.

A Christian named John knew in his heart that the violence of this world would not triumph.

He wrote of his vision: "I saw a new heaven and a new earth – and a new Jerusalem coming down from heaven.

"In that place that is to come, there will be no more death, no more grief, or crying or pain.

"Jesus will welcome into the city those who have accepted his invitation to life.

"They will live for ever there, in the light of God.

"So be it. Come, Lord Jesus!"